SYMBOLIC COMMUNICATION
IN LATE MEDIEVAL TOWNS

ML

MEDIAEVALIA LOVANIENSIA

Editorial Board

SERIES I / STUDIA XXXVII

KATHOLIEKE UNIVERSITEIT LEUVEN
INSTITUUT VOOR MIDDELEEUWSE STUDIES
LEUVEN (BELGIUM)

SYMBOLIC COMMUNICATION
IN LATE MEDIEVAL TOWNS

Edited by

Jacoba VAN LEEUWEN

1425

LEUVEN UNIVERSITY PRESS

2006

ISBN 90 5867 522 X
ISBN 978-90-5867-522-4
D/2006/1869/5
NUR: 684, 694

CONTENTS

INTRODUCTION

by

Jacoba VAN LEEUWEN

Symbolic communication in medieval studies

In *Moderne Mediävistik* (1999), Hans-Werner Goetz pointed out that during the previous decade historians had paid increasing attention to the communication of medieval power. It was not power itself that was analysed. Rather, the emphasis was placed on the representation: the performance or the staging of power. Rituals, ceremonies, gestures, symbols and signs were the material the historian had to work with; sociology and anthropology provided the methodology to interpret these phenomena.[1]

This recent interest in symbolic communication cannot be labelled a true turn, be a cultural, symbolic or performative one. Research in this field is indeed rooted in the work of much older scholars such as Huizinga and Burckhart.[2] Moreover, in the fifties, Schramm and Kantorowicz approached coronations and other royal ceremonies as forms of symbolic performances of royal power.[3] In France, members of the *Annales* school applied anthropological research to a medieval context; Bloch, for example, analysed the symbolic power of French kings[4] and Le Goff studied feudal rituals.[5] Quite often anthropology inspired the historian to explore new questions. The *rite de passage*, defined by Van Gennep[6] and elaborated by Turner,[7] is just one example of such a suc-

---

1. Hans-Werner Goetz, *Moderne Mediävistik. Stand und Perspektiven der Mittelalterforschung* (Darmstadt, 1999), pp. 212-216.
2. Johan Huizinga, *Herfsttij der middeleeuwen. Studie over levens- en gedachtenvormen der veertiende en vijftiende eeuw in Frankrijk en de Nederlanden*, 21st edition (Amsterdam, 1997); Jacob Burckhardt, *Die Cultur der Renaissance in Italien* (1860).
3. Ernst Kantorowicz, *The Kings two Bodies. A Study in Medieval Political Theology* (Princeton, 1957); Percy Ernst Schramm, *Herrschaftszeichen und Staatssymbolik: Beiträge zu ihrer Geschichte vom dritten bis zum sechzehnten Jahrhundert*, Monumenta Germaniae Historica, Schriften 13, 3 vols. (Stuttgart, 1954-1956).
4. Marc Bloch, *Les rois thaumaturges. Étude sur le caractère surnaturel attribué à la puissance royale particulièrement en France et en Angleterre,* Bibliothèque des Histoires (Paris, 1983).
5. Jaques Le Goff, 'Le rituel symbolique de la vassalité', in Jacques Le Goff ed., *Pour un autre moyen âge* (Paris, 1977), pp. 349-420.
6. Arnold Van Gennep, *Les rites de passage. Etude systematique des rites* (Paris, 1909).
7. Victor Turner, *The Ritual Process. Structure and Antistructure* (Chicago, 1975); Victor Turner, *Dramas, Fields and Metaphors. Symbolic Action in Human Society* (London, 1990).

cessful theory. The thesis of Geertz on the *Theatre State* in nineteenth-century Bali[8] was also adopted by many medievalists. The studies written by Davis,[9] Trexler[10] and Gurevic[11] were forerunners of the present interest in ritual studies.

In short, research into the medieval uses of symbols and rituals is not new. However, during the last decade this domain has indeed been addressed more systematically.

Firstly, the theoretical backgrounds of ritual behaviour were explored more intensively. Buc, Alhoff, Muir and others pointed out that the methodology used in sociology and anthropology cannot easily be applied to medieval source material. Therefore, they developed a specific set of questions and methods that the medievalist should employ when studying past forms of symbolic communication.[12] In this volume, Brown also explores the use of models from anthropology and their possible application to the study of late medieval urban rituals.

Secondly, the research in this domain was institutionalised into several research units. In Münster, the *Graduiertenkolleg 'Gesellschaftliche Symbolik im Mittelalter'* and the *Sonderforschungsbereich 'Symbolische Kommunikation und gesellschaftliche Wertesysteme'"* study these phenomena in a truly interdisciplinary way. In Zurich, the use of different media of communication is being studied in a large project entitled *'Medienwandel in vorindustriellen Zeit'*. Recently, the Sonderforschungsbereich *'Kulturen des performativen'* at the Freie Universität Berlin has begun analysing rituals as performances: staged arrangements of power.

In addition to these projects, many researchers have been inspired by this rediscovery of ritual behaviour. Since almost every human action has symbolic implications, a wide range of subjects has been studied.

8. Clifford Geertz, *Negara. The Theatre State in Nineteenth-Century Bali* (Princeton, 1980). In this volume, Andrew Brown analyses the use of this theory for medieval studies.

9. Natalie Davis Zemon, *Society and Culture in Early Modern France* (London, 1975); Natalie Davis Zemon, *The gift in sixteenth-century France*, The Curti lectures (Madison, Wisc., 2000).

10. Richard Trexler, *Public Life in Renaissance Florence* (New York, 1980); Richard Trexler, 'Follow the Flag. The Ciompi Revolt Seen from the Streets', in *Bibliothèque d'Humanisme et Renaissance,* 46 (1984), pp. 357-392.

11. Aron Guerevic, *Historical Anthropology of the Middle Ages* (Cambridge, 1992).

12. Philippe Buc, *The Dangers of Ritual. Between Early Medieval Texts and Social Scientific Theory* (Princeton, 2002); Gerd Althoff, 'Zur Bedeutung symbolischer Kommunikation für das Verständnis des Mittelalters', in *Frühmittelalterliche Studien,* 31 (1997), pp. 370-389; Edward Muir, *Civic Ritual in Renaissance Venice* (Princeton, 1981).

This introduction, however, does not seek to provide an overview of the large number of publications in this field. What we wish to do is to explore a number of methodological problems the medievalist is faced with: the definition of symbolic communication, the interaction between tradition and innovation, and the perception of medieval rituals.

The definitions of symbolic communication

Communication can be defined quite easily as every form of mutual exchange of information in consciously encoded messages. These messages can be communicated with varying degrees of directness. Moreover, several media can be used, both verbal and non-verbal. Communication thus presupposes a sender, a receiver and a code.[13]

According to Althoff, one can discern three types of communication in the Middle Ages: oral, written and symbolic. The latter is defined as those forms of communication in which the message is expressed in an indirect way: the meaning surpasses the immediate recognition; the message is ambiguous and hidden. This symbolic communication employs signs and symbols with a specific meaning; it demonstrates the message as opposed to other forms of communication that provide and explain information.[14]

I doubt whether it is necessary to clearly discern such a specific form of communication, since almost every exchange of information has symbolic implications: a code is used to transmit a message each time, and it is up to the receiver to decode it. Can one truly speak of a meaningful difference between immediate and indirect communication? Perhaps the visual demonstration of social order was in a way more direct than a written treatise on these relationships: an image can say more than many words.

13. Marco Mostert, 'New Approaches to Medieval Communication?', in Marco Mostert ed., *New approaches to medieval Communication,* Utrecht Studies in Medieval Literacy, I (Turnhout, 1999), pp. 18-21; Gerd Althoff and Ludwig Siep, 'Symbolische Kommunikation und gesellschaftliche Wertesysteme vom Mittelalter bis zur französischen Revolution. Der neue Münsterer Sonderforschungsbereich 496', in *Frühmittelalterliche Studien,* 34 (2000) p. 395.

14. Gerd Althoff, 'Zur Bedeutung', p. 373: 'Vielmehr scheint es sinnvoll zu sein, drei Bereiche mittelalterlicher Kommunikation zu unterscheiden: die verbale, die schriftliche und die symbolische, die zumeist nonverbal durch Zeichen aller art Nachrichten und Informationen vermittelt.'

In addition, can one truly discern a separate verbal and a non-verbal form of communication? Are not both aspects always closely connected, especially in medieval times? The concept of 'symbolic communication' suggests that every element of this communication is symbolic, which, in most cases, is not true. Rituals and ceremonies often combine statutory acts and the communication about these formal events.[15] Moreover, several media are combined to communicate a message, but not all of them can be labelled a symbol or an 'indirect' form of communication.

Althoff indeed mentions that the three forms of communication he cites sometimes overlap, and that words and texts can be used in rituals as well. He tries to circumvent this question by arguing that symbolic communication was dominant in the Middle Ages,[16] a statement that – in my view – again shows that one might question the existence of an isolated form of symbolic communication in which all elements are symbolic.

Althoff and Siep also state that a strict definition of symbolic communication should not be given, and they therefore also speak of 'symbolic components of communication'.[17] Perhaps it is indeed better to speak of communication that uses symbols and thus places the emphasis on the media that are used. However, this poses a new problem, since the concept of a symbol is not clear. Historians speak of symbols and signs, acts and gestures, without clearly defining these concepts. The word 'ritual' is used to describe many phenomena. However, it is usually defined as a 'chain of symbolic actions', and thus is just as unclear. Philippe Buc even called it a dangerous word that is better forgotten. The reason why these concepts are not strictly determined is that historians usually do not want to paste a modern theory onto the medieval past. This results in the concepts they use being rather vague and imprecise. Moreover, as Buc has clearly demonstrated, the use of a word like 'ritual' implies hidden associations.[18] Of course, one cannot truly escape these problems and create a completely new terminology. We will continue to speak of symbols, signs and rituals, but should be aware of the vagueness inherent in these concepts. One should be more careful about

15. Wim Blockmans and Esther Donckers, 'Self-Representation of Court and City in Flanders and Brabant in the Fifteenth and Early Sixteenth Centuries', in Wim Blockmans and Anteun Janse, eds., *Showing Status. Representation of Social Positions in the Late Middle Ages,* Medieval Texts and Cultures of Northern Europe, 2 (Turnhout, 1999), pp. 87-89.
16. Gerd Althoff, 'Zur Bedeutung', p. 373.
17. Gerd Althoff and Ludwig Siep, 'Symbolische Kommunikation', p. 396.
18. Philippe Buc, *The Dangers of Ritual,* p. 247.

using the adjective 'symbolic' and more precise regarding how a certain gesture, act or medium refers to a deeper meaning.

What I want to demonstrate here is that the concept of symbolic communication is rather vague, like the concepts 'ritual', 'sign' and 'symbol'. Symbolic communication can be applied to almost every exchange of information and every human action. Perhaps it would be better to speak of communication with symbols, and to study the use of various communication media and the ways in which they were combined. Thus, one can discern verbal and non-verbal media and their interaction. One can attribute symbolic meaning to these media within the entire context of the communication act, without stating that every element of the communication is symbolic. In this case, rituals are not forms of symbolic communication, but a form of communication that uses symbols – like objects, speech-acts and visual media – in combination with more direct forms of communication.

Tradition and innovation

Nowadays, historians conceive rituals as a form of communication in which messages are sent to an audience. Recently Buc, Althoff and Koziol[19] successfully argued that such actions were not at all an irrational routine. Unlike the rituals studied by anthropologists in primitive societies, medieval rituals were political instruments applied intentionally to obtain a certain effect. As Althoff puts it, rituals were like the rules of a game that were creatively employed in each individual situation.[20]

Although rituals have – as Koziol put it – an 'aura of changelessness', their authors played creatively with tradition and innovation. On the one hand, recognizability and repeatability were of major importance. Thus, the organiser based his actions on traditions and customs that constituted the rules of the ritual. On the other hand, he adapted the customary scenario to the specific context in which it was used. It was of the utmost importance that the limits of its recognizability were not crossed: whenever the balance between tradition and innovation was disturbed, the ritual lost its strength.[21]

19. Geoffrey Koziol, *Begging Pardon and Favor. Ritual and Political Order in Early Medieval France* (London, 1992).
20. Gerd Althoff, 'The Variability of Rituals in the Middle Ages', in Gerd Althoff, Joannes Fried, Patrick Geary, eds., *Medieval Concepts of the Past. Ritual, Memory, Historiography* (Cambridge, 2002), pp. 71-88.
21. Geoffrey Koziol, *Begging Pardon and Favor*, pp. 292-293.

Recently, Plesch and Ashley have drawn attention to 'The cultural processes of Appropriation'. According to their view, appropriation is closely connected with concepts like 'influence' and 'intertextuality', but can be clearly distinguished from them, since appropriation – and I quote – 'emphasises the act of taking, it is understood to be active, subjective and motivated'. It is not just borrowing something or being influenced by something, but it stresses the motivation for this process: to gain power over something (an idea, a tradition...). Appropriation reuses existing material and essentially generates new meanings in the new context in which this material is used: traditions, spaces, artefacts, ideas etc. are 'brought to represent something different from their original purposes'. New layers of meaning were added to reused material. The historian should always pay attention to the dialogue between the various layers of meaning. Was there for instance a strong contrast between the old and the new meaning, purpose or use? Was the original meaning completely retained? Between these two extremes lies a wide range of possible combinations.[22]

Michel de Certeau is missing from the great number of scholars that Plesch and Ashley cite. However, his observations on the 'tactics of practice' do correspond quite well to their theory of appropriation. De Cerreau argues that symbolic actions might look traditional from the outside, but that well-known gestures might conceal new meanings, since they are used in a new context by new groups. The reuse and even manipulation of existing material was thus significant for the 'tactics of practice'. He argued that such creative reuse of elements is in present-day society typical for the weak and the powerless who thus demonstrate their resistance. However, he stated that in the Middle Ages this 'tactic' was also used by the powerful to demonstrate their power.[23]

Each time a message is sent, the author of the message creates a 'present', based on past traditions, which aims toward the future.[24] From a methodological perspective, this means that the medievalist should analyse the 'archaeology of tradition': all the information contained in each performance of the ritual should be gathered; thus one might discern that which is unique and typical for each performance.[25]

22. Véronique Plesch and Kathleen Ashley, 'The Cultural Processes of Appropriation', *Journal of Medieval and Early Modern Studies*, 5 (2002), pp. 1-15.
23. Michel de Certeau, *The Practice of Everyday Life* (Berkeley, 1984), pp. xix and 37
24. Gerd Althoff and Ludwig Siep, 'Symbolische Kommunikation', p. 403.
25. Gerd Althoff, 'Zur Bedeutung', pp. 370-389.

However, such an inventory does not suffice, since the tradition's meaning was not stable but rather changed over time. Sometimes a ritual only outwardly looks traditional, but the meaning has completely changed.[26] Althoff therefore pleads for a concise 'history of signs' in which the medievalist seeks to explore how a sign or a symbol was used in various contexts and how its meaning and interpretation had changed. The transmission of a symbol or a tradition from one context to another should be analysed. Why was a tradition appropriated, and which associations with its origins were implied? Thus, the medievalist should ask why and when traditions were transmitted, changed or even abolished[27].

Therefore, I do not think that it is fruitful to speak of the core and the margins of a ritual as Koziol does. He stated that the core consisted of those components that were necessary for the action's recognizability and legitimacy. The margin contained those elements that could be changed easily without endangering the stability of the ritual.[28] Since each performance of a ritual was a new creation, every aspect of the performance was reused and actualised. Thus, the core could also achieve a new meaning. In my view, a more fruitful way to deal with this tension between tradition and innovation is Althoff's concept of an 'ideal type of ritual'. This ideal type exists in the mind of both actors and spectators, and 'takes on a material form that is easily recognised in its various concrete manifestations'.[29]

Perception

Communication presupposes a receiver. An audience receives the message that is sent; it decodes and interprets the information. Moreover, the making public of the actions has a binding effect, both for the sender and for the receiver.

This does not mean, however, that an audience witnesses all the phases of the event. Often one can detect an alternation between open and closed phases of the event: not all the phases are open to every group. In the process of electing a new town government, for instance, a

---

26. David Cannadine, 'The Context, Performance and Meaning of Ritual: the Britisch Monarchy and the Invention of Tradition', in Eric Hobsbawm and Terence Ranger, eds., *The Invention of Tradition* (Cambridge, 1983), p. 105.

27. Gerd Althoff, 'Zur Bedeutung', pp. 386-387; Gerd Althoff, 'The Variability', p. 75.

28. Geoffrey Koziol, *Begging Pardon and Favor*, p. 296.

29. Gerd Althoff, 'The Variability', p. 71.

conclave was organised. The secrecy of this phase communicated the fact that the election was pure and that no external influences could corrupt the board of electors.[30] In other cases, the exclusion of certain groups underlined the distinction between participants and non-participants.[31]

The audience did not play a passive role. Often the witnesses of the event were expected to participate. They had to confirm their support in an acclamation or participate even more actively. During royal entries and after proclamations of peace, for example, the inhabitants of the town were urged to organise theatre plays, fireworks and decorations. In organising such events, existing tensions between various social groups were canalised; the town thus presented a picture of civic unity. However, such reciprocity between sender and audience was often only superficial, since it was organised entirely by the governors and not based on the spontaneous response of the town's inhabitants.[32]

Buc has underlined that this audience was always a risk for the author, since he could never predict how the receivers of his message would respond. The author depended on the reactions of his public, since their interpretation determined the success of his actions. The sender of the message could fail if his message was not understood or if his message was questioned and even rejected. Thus, rituals did not simply create legitimacy or stability, but rather always depended upon the reactions of the audience.[33]

Since the response of the vast and often anonymous crowd of spectators could not be controlled, the sender had to encode his message care-

30. Dietrich Poeck, 'Zahl, Tag und Stuhl. Zur Semiotik der Ratswahl', in *Frühmittelalterliche Studien*, 33 (1999), pp. 396-427.
31. Michael Bojcov, 'Qualitäten des Raumes in zeremoniellen Situationen: Das Heilige Römische Reich, 14-15. Jahrhundert', in Werner Paravicini ed., *Zeremoniell und Raum. 4. Symposium der Residenzen-Kommission der Akademie der Wissenschaften in Göttingen veranstaltet gemeinsam mit dem Deutschen Historischen Institut Paris und dem Historischen Institut der Universität Potsdam. Potsdam 25. bis 27. September 1994.* Residenzenforschung. Herausgegeben von der Residenzen-Kommission der Akademie der Wissenschaften in Göttingen, 6 (Sigmaringen, 1997), p. 147; Klaus Scheiner, 'Texte, Bilder, Rituale. Fragen und Erträge einer Sektion auf dem Deutschen Historikertag (8. bis 11. September 1998', in Klaus Schreiner and Gabriella Signori, eds., *Bilder, Texte, Rituale. Wirklichkeitsbezug und Wirklichkeitskonstruktion politisch-rechtlicher Kommunikationsmedien in Stadt und Adelsgesellschaften des späten Mittelalters,* Zeitschrift für historische Forschung, Beiheft 14 (Berlin, 2000), p. 7.
32. Wim Blockmans and Esther Donckers, 'Self representation', p. 88.
33. Philippe Buc, *The Dangers of Rituals*, pp. 8-9; Geoffrey Koziol, *Begging Pardon and Favor*, p. 310.

fully. As stated earlier, he could employ traditions that the audience knew. Thus, the sender presupposed that the witnesses knew the meaning of the symbols he employed.[34] On the other hand, a sender could also exclude an audience by the subtle use of codes: by using several layers of meaning, some audiences would have access to all the associations made, while these meanings would remain concealed for other groups. Thus, the actual and true meaning of a ritual could be concealed for some groups and accessible for others.[35]

Although the perception of the audience was of major importance for the success of a ritual, it is not easy to retrace the way audiences have understood these events. In theory, audiences could respond, but the sources often do not describe their reactions and pay little attention to them. The lack of information available concerning the response of the audience does not necessarily mean that the witnesses agreed or that they understood the message. Perhaps they were not interested, or were unable to question the communication. Or, perhaps they understood something in a completely different way than the sender intended. During a crisis, when communication failed, more information could be found about the audience. Crowds sometimes revolted against the sender of the message. Of course, these are exceptional events, but they do give us some insights into the way audiences interpreted messages that were communicated to them.

In short, the source-material presents a significant problem. We cannot truly study the ritual practice, but must rely on medieval sources *describing* these events. The authors of these sources have selected the material and, in their turn, encoded the message they wanted to send to their readers. Buc has clearly demonstrated that sources always offer an interpretation of the ritual, a perception of what has happened. A medievalist should therefore always keep in mind that the sources he uses are produced in a precise context and with a specific purpose. Buc therefore pleads for a 'contextual and site-specific approach' that does justice to the strategies employed by the authors of these texts.[36]

The medievalist should be aware of the vast expansion of meanings associated with an act of communication. Firstly, the sender has encoded

---

34. Gerd Althoff, 'Die Kultur der Zeichen und Symbole', in *Frühmittelalterliche Studien,* 36 (2002), pp. 7-8.
35. Véronique Plesch and Kathleen Ashley, 'The Cultural Processes of Appropriation', p. 5.
36. Philippe Buc, *The Danger of Rituals,* p. 251-252.

the message with several layers of meaning. Secondly, the receiver may
have added new and even very different interpretations of the message
sent. Thirdly, the medieval authors had their reasons for composing a
description of the event. The medievalist should bear all of these layers
of perception in mind.

The late medieval town and the entanglement of civic and princely symbolic actions

The essays in this volume all address, in one way or another, symbolic
forms of communication in the late medieval town. The focus is placed
on two areas that were highly urbanised in late medieval times: the Low
Countries, including the towns of northern France, and the Swiss Confederation. Even though the political context in which the towns functioned was quite different, both areas were known for their wealthy
towns that had obtained a high degree of autonomous power over their
rulers. In the late medieval context of centralisation, tensions with higher
levels of power were threatening this independence. The often quite
elaborate political history of these towns is reflected in many sources
that offer detailed information about the use of symbolic means of communication combined with, or opposed to, the use of literacy. Indeed, at
the end of the Middle Ages, ritual behaviour was not reduced to routine
jobs that did not really matter, but on the contrary was employed in a
highly sophisticated manner in order to efficiently legitimise the power
position of various parties. It is in comparing both areas that we can see
how a particular political context has influenced the use of symbolic
forms of communication and has brought about a rereading of old traditions.

The contributions in this volume all offer case studies of the 'tactics
of practise' and deal with the various ways in which symbols and traditions were appropriated in new settings. How were new layers of meaning attached to well-known traditions? And what were the restrictions of
such appropriations, or put otherwise, when was recognizability so damaged that a ritual was no longer understood? This volume might suggest
a strict opposition between civic and princely ritual behaviour. Indeed,
three articles are concerned with the public encounters between rulers
and town dwellers, while three others deal with the appropriation of traditions to express the political and religious relations between the various social groups within the towns. At the same time, however, all the
contributions demonstrate that such a clear distinction between princely

and local traditions in fact did not truly exist. Both rulers and towns were using, reusing and even abusing each other's symbols of power. Thus, the quite intense exchange between civic and court ritual makes it impossible to speak of an opposition between purely urban and purely princely symbolic actions. In reality, various layers of meaning were attached to existing traditions, and both rulers and towns reinvented symbols in order to convince their audiences of the legitimacy of their position.

As stated, three articles deals with symbolic events that were organised to address a ruler. These public encounters were not spontaneous meetings, but were carefully planned so as to reflect the current balance between the various levels of power. Quite often representatives of the town and the court worked together to achieve a spectacle that was understood both by ruler and ruled, in order to reflect the divine harmony of political relations. On other occasions, one of the parties could set up a ritual on its own in order to impose its interpretation of the symbolic tradition on the adversary.

Andrew Brown reflects on the way in which the rulers of Flanders used ritual in the government of their cities. The employment of means of mass communication in order to tighten the ruler's grip on urban society is demonstrated by a detailed study on ritual in medieval Bruges. The manipulation of civic traditions to make symbolic statements about princely power is one of the main themes of this argument. In this context, Brown searches for ritual models to explain the Burgundian context. He therefore digresses into more theoretical questions, like the way rituals are related to political power and reflect social order, and the risks and restrictions of the entanglement of princely and civic traditions. The use of the concept of the Theatre State as defined by Geertz for the medieval town is questioned and thus the author compares the late medieval rituals with other, less known anthropological models. This theoretical context is then compared with three important ceremonies to mark the ritual year in late medieval Bruges: the Holy Blood procession, the General Procession, and the Jousts of the White Bear. They were all civic-based and drew in the rulers of Flanders in particular ways. A concise analysis of these rituals demonstrates how civic and courtly interpretations of symbolic actions were often entangled.

Christoph Weber also reflects on encounters of rulers and ruled in analysing the political relations between a town and its bishop. In his contribution on rituals in medieval Basel, he discusses the statement that from the fourteenth century onwards such public encounters ended up in empty formalism and became nothing more than routine jobs. Weber, on the contrary, argues that the use of such encounters in a particular historical context does show significant transitions and that therefore these encounters had not lost their importance at all. The annual election of the local community is the starting point of his examination. In the conflictual context of late medieval Basel, both the bishop and the town appropriated the existing traditions to legitimise their power position and to humiliate their opponent. This contribution clearly demonstrates that the growth of literacy did not end the use of ritual behaviour but could in fact be the direct cause for the development of complex modes of action in which literacy and performances interacted. Especially underlined are the symbolic functions of the charters as significant means to symbolise power.

Both Brown and Weber stress the importance of the perception of the appropriation of traditions. Brown pointed out that large pageants involving a crowd were always open to alternative interpretations or even to misrecognition. The same symbol, like a relic, could bear several meanings for several groups. Weber points out that the bishop and the town of Basel interpreted the same ritual traditions in a completely different way, and that this divergence of meaning caused tensions and conflicts. Organisers were often quite aware of the possibility that various groups added their own layers of meaning to a symbolic object or event. Therefore, they could set up a complex communication strategy in order to reach different categories of audience at the same time.

Katell Lavéant demonstrates that the Royal Entry of Elenor of Habsburg in Abbeville (1531) was staged with great care in order to involve a divergent range of audiences in the town. The message was conveyed in a dialogue by allegorical characters that represented one or more groups who were witnessing the play, in order to invite them to become personally involved in the event. However surprising some of these identifications must have been, the organisers in fact transformed the existing system and scrupulously observed the older tradition. As such, the familiarity of the event was preserved so that the audience seems not to have been disturbed by what was represented on stage.

The three other contributions deal with the use of symbolic actions to express political relations within towns. These three case studies explore how the balance between the various social groups living inside the town walls could be expressed or threatened by ritual behaviour. The

flexibility of traditions in a rapidly changing political context is demonstrated by the creativeness of municipal governors and rebels in adapting
existing patterns of action to serve their own goals.

In his study of late medieval Leiden, Damen sketches the functions of
ritual wine pouring in the political and religious context of this Dutch
town. The delicate use of these gifts to communicate power and prestige
within the town and to officials from abroad is explored. As was also the
case in Swiss towns, these gifts were not considered bribery, because
they served well-defined political goals. In fact, they were often considered a good 'investment' since they implied reciprocal gifts from the
beneficiaries. As such, a network of interdependence was created that
was legitimated by the common good of the town. Damen approaches
this theme via a quantitative study of the various beneficiaries of the
wine gifts in medieval Leiden. He analyses the political use of these gifts
over a period of 160 years. Thus, this contribution succeeds in demonstrating both the establishment of a tradition and the way the symbolic
meanings of the wine jugs evolved over time. Significant changes in the
use and functions of these gifts are detected and explained within their
historical context.

The influence of a changing historical context on the use of traditions
is also explored in my contribution to this volume. This study focuses on
the changes the ritual election and installation of aldermen underwent
during an important urban uprising in 1488. More specifically, the delicate mixture between the established traditions of this yearly event in
Bruges and the rites of rebellion is analysed. In 1488, the rebels were
interested in legitimising the political status of the newly elected aldermen whom they had installed. In order to claim legitimacy, many traditional means were employed to stress the familiarity of the event and
thus to guarantee the credibility of their actions. Other aspects of the
1488 ceremony were appropriated from the rites of rebellion and thus
were new to the context of the election-ritual. The risks and limits of
such a new addition to a well-known ritual were observed with care. In
the end, the true change in power in the town was performed separately,
instead of integrating it into the traditional solemnity, since this change
would otherwise have damaged the ritual's recognizability too much.

Michael Jucker also deals with conflicts and tensions within a rebellious town. In his contribution, the settlement of conflicts by medieval
diplomacy is explored in the study of one particular crisis: the uprising
of Zurich against Hans Waldmann, a mayor accused of bribery and other
violations of the commune's common good. Jucker focuses on the flex-

ibility of the communication strategies employed by the parties in a conflict. Besides the use of written documents to solve the conflict, various signs, gestures and symbols were employed. Although both sides of the conflict used symbolic language, the meaning of their actions could be ambiguously interpreted or even completely misunderstood. Thus, the mediators were obliged to study the meaning of signs in order to be able to judge the symbolic impact of the actions correctly. Therefore, they had to deal with the delicate mixture of tradition, innovation and perception of symbolic forms of communication in a late medieval town.

This volume is the result of an international workshop that was organised in Leuven in November 2003. On this occasion, nine young researchers presented their work in progress on the symbolic aspects of communication in the late medieval town. I would like to thank the Dutch *Onderzoekschool Medievistiek* for giving us the opportunity to organise this gathering and for funding the publication of these proceedings. I am also very obliged to the *Department of History* and the *Institute of Medieval Studies* of the *K.U. Leuven* who have supported this initiative and agreed to publish this volume in the series Mediaevalia Lovaniensia. I am much indebted to Professor Werner Verbeke for all his support over the last two years.

Katholieke Universiteit Leuven

Andrew BROWN

RITUAL AND STATE-BUILDING:
CEREMONIES IN LATE MEDIEVAL BRUGES

Communication between rulers and ruled, however symbolic, came with
a price tag. The arrival in Bruges on 14 April 1457 of three rulers, Duke
Philip the Good, his son Charles, and the dauphin Louis (while in rebellion against his father King Charles VII), put the citizens to some considerable expense.[1] According to a local chronicler, the visitors were received
in 'great triumph' outside the Boeverie gate by the magistrates, principal
citizens, and the craft guilds, all in costly dress; the city spent over 400
livres parisis on cloth, trumpets and torches at the gate, on *tableaux vivants*
along the streets, and fires in the *burg*; and over 1100 *livres* on three gold
and silver vessels, on wine and wax, as gifts for the dauphin. His stay in
Bruges during May, required the city to open its coffers more widely than
normal: 745 *livres* were disgorged to stage the annual jousting event of the
White Bear on 2 May; on the following day, for the annual procession of
the Holy Blood relic, the city magistrates ordered an 'excellent procession'
with gold crosses and plays which more than double the usual amount was
spent.[2] The dauphin 'greatly wondered' at the wealth on display. Charles
(*le travaillant*) worked hard at imposing on the minds of citizens and
dauphin a similar impression about himself. He personally took part in the
White Bear jousts at which he evidently hoped to shine – not just by spend-
ing at least 650 *livres tournois* on cloth, jewels, horses and lances to take
part, but also by arranging a discrete practice session outside the town a few
days before the event.[3] He also had a special platform constructed along the

   * I am very grateful to the British Academy for a travel research grant which enabled
me to complete research for this article.

   1. For the following, see the description in a local chronicle (Stadsbiblioteek, Bruges,
Handschriften, 436, fols. 235r-35v; and city expenditure in the Stadsarchief, Bruges [hence-
forward SAB] 216: 1456/7, fols. 30r, 51r- 53v.
   2. The usual amounts spent in the 1450s by the town on the Holy Blood for painting
work for 'plays' had been 100 *livres*; and on the White Bear (on average) c.600 *livres*
(SAB, 216, 1450-56).
   3. Archives départementales du Nord, Lille, [henceforward ADN] B 3661, fols. 34r-
44v, 68r (for '12s paid for a house where the count armed himself on the day he went to
try out a horse outside the town in order to joust on the following Sunday,' see ibid,
fol. 38r).

Steenstraat so that he and the dauphin could watch the procession of the Holy Blood as the cortège passed by.[4]

Wonder had not been the only emotion experienced by the dauphin in Bruges. According to Chastellain, the dauphin's reaction to an incident prior to his Entry outside the city gate had been embarrassingly close to terror: the enthusiastic advance of two groups of foreign merchants towards him, their unlit torches mistaken for lances, had temporarily deprived him of movement and speech.[5] Inside the city Louis's eye may have been caught by spectacles other than those paid for by the city. Chastellain covered the event rather differently from the local chronicler, reserving detailed description for the *tableaux* arranged by the foreign merchants in Bruges (and the dauphin's reaction to them during his Entry), rather than for the *tableaux* put on by the craft guilds (or those prepared for the Holy Blood procession).[6] In the long run, if the dauphin was ever dazzled by what he saw of Bruges and of Charles in 1457, the effects quickly wore off. Cordiality turned into hostility, and by July 1465, Charles was leading an army into France against Louis. An inconclusive battle was fought at Montlhéry. A month or so later, the Bruges authorities were required to take the Holy Blood relic on a special procession as thanksgiving for Charles's 'victory' against the French.[7]

State Power and the 'Theatre-State'

Montlhéry marked an important stage in Charles's assertion of Burgundian independence from French sovereignty; and his use of the Holy

---

4. ADN, Recette générale de Flandre, B 4104, fol. 104 (at the cost of 76 *livres tournois*).

5. Georges Chastellain, *Chroniques,* ed. M. le Baron Kervyn de Lettenhove, III (Brussels, 1864), p. 303.

6. *Ibid.,* pp. 301-6, 309-10. Although Chastellain ignores the *tableaux* also put on by the craft guilds, these had evidently been required to make considerable contributions to the whole event: for instance, in 1461 the coopers petitioned the city authorities to be allowed to put up membership fees because of the 'great costs' that had been incurred on Holy Blood day and at the recent 'Blijde Incomst' (SAB, 96, Groenenbouc A, fol. 231v). Chastellain also describes the jousting as an event that was solely the result of Charles's initiative.

7. Nicolaes Despars, *Cronycke van Vlaenderen ende graefscepe van Vlaenderen...van jaeren 1405-1492,* ed. J. de Jonghe (Bruges, 1829-40), III, p. 568. The town accounts do not refer directly to payments for this; and confusingly a more contemporary chronicler than Despars refers to this procession as having carried the 'sacrament' (HS, 436, fol. 238r); as do the chapter act-books of St Donatian (Bisschopelijk archief, Bruges [henceforward BAB], A 53, fol. 155v). But the fabric accounts of St Jacob's church refer to bell ringing 'als men processie general drouch metten Heleghen Bloede' (Rijksarchief, Bruges [henceforward RAB], Oud kerkarchief Sint Jacob 24, 1464/5, fol. 83v).

Blood and other ceremonies in Bruges might be viewed as part of his state-building efforts. The way in which the rulers of Flanders used 'ritual' in the government of their cities is the subject of this contribution. Recent research into symbolic communication between rulers and ruled has opened up new perspectives on events like the dauphin's visit to Bruges; toes have been gingerly dipped into the interdisciplinary waters of anthropological study to refresh research into late medieval ceremony. The work of the anthropologist Clifford Geertz (amongst others) has often provided a springboard for departure: his emphasis on symbols as an integral part of the political process (as social facts integral to, rather than independent of, systems of power relations) is applauded as a means to integrate the study of late medieval ceremonies with commentary on political and social events.[8]

It has also provided the means to develop a theme that has traditionally dominated the historiography of the Low Countries: the growth of state power. There used to be a tendency to search for the origins of modern Belgium or Holland in the medieval period when neither nation-state existed, and to locate promising premonitions of national self-consciousness in the struggles of native cities (usually Dutch-speaking) against their (French-speaking) foreign rulers.[9] If more modern analyses are no longer crudely teleological in approach, there remains a strong tendency when writing about the period to prioritize the expanding hegemony – political, economic, social and cultural – of state over city. The Valois Burgundian dukes are seen as importing French ideas of sovereignty to curtail the independence of native cities;[10] simultaneously they made increasing use of spectacle and ceremony to 'strengthen authority'. Thus the magnificence of Burgundian ceremony grew 'in tandem with the grad-

---

8. Peter Arnade, *Realms of Ritual: Burgundian Ceremony and Civic Life in Late Medieval Ghent* (New York, 1996), pp. 4-5; Wim Blockmans and Esther Donckers, 'Self-Representation of Court and City in Flanders and Brabant in the fifteenth and early sixteenth centuries', in *Showing Status. Representations of Social Positions in the Late Middle Ages*, eds. Wim Blockmans and Antheun Janse (Turnhout, 1999), p. 110.

9. For an excellent exposure of this trend, see Malcolm Vale, *The Princely Court. Medieval Courts and Culture in North-West Europe, 1270-1380* (Oxford, 2001), esp. pp. 295-6. And for the most celebrated example of the trend see: Henri Pirenne, *Early Democracies in the Low Countries: Urban Society and Political Conflict in the Middle Ages and Renaissance* (New York, 1963), esp. pp. 29-40. As Marc Boone laconically remarks on urban historiography in medieval Flanders: 'in the beginning was the word, and the word was Pirenne' (Marc Boone, 'Urban Space and the Political Context in Late Medieval Flanders', *Journal of Interdisciplinary History,* 24:4 (2002), 621).

10. *Ibid.*, 633; Marc Boone, 'La justice en spectacle. La justice urbaine en Flandre et la crise du pouvoir 'bourgignonne' (1477-1488)', *Revue historique,* 308 (2003), 44.

ual scaling back of civic political rights'; ceremony was a 'vital idiom in an all-important struggle between city and state'.[11] Particular ceremonies, like the procession, have been viewed as a means of mass communication which princes increasingly used in the late medieval period to tighten their grip on urban society: ritual was a 'cheaper way' than repression to curb urban unrest.[12]

The value of this approach is undoubted: serious conflicts between prince and citizens (even in Bruges) did take place throughout the period; and as prosopographical studies and investigations into civic finances have shown, members of the civic elites were certainly drawn into the expanding bureaucracy of their rulers and could side with them against more popular elements within cities.[13] Some studies use rather loaded terms to describe the process: these civic 'elites', anxious to line their own pockets and advance themselves socially, become 'clients' 'complicit' in Burgundian state-building. But they do reveal how complex and divided the urban environment was; and the implication we might draw is that use of ritual to control such environments was also likely to be complex.

Important insights have been afforded into what kinds of ritual worked best in the attempt to impose political control. Clearly the process required use of existing traditions. Elements of the Church liturgy – and the use of sacred light – were made to serve the ideological ends of the ruler.[14] Civic traditions could be manipulated to make symbolic statements about princely power – especially, for instance, in those entry ceremonies, paid for out of civic resources, which involved the public humiliation of citi-

---

11. Peter Arnade, 'City, State and Public Ritual in the Late Medieval Burgundian Netherlands', *Comparative Studies in Society and History,* 39 (1997), 309, 317.

12. Blockmans and Donckers, 'Self-Representation', p. 82. See also Martha Howell for comment (amongst other things) on the 'struggle for hegemony' over urban space between city and prince ('The Spaces of Late Medieval Urbanity', in *Shaping Urban Identity in Late Medieval Europe,* eds. Marc Boone and Peter Stabel (Leuven, 2000), p. 18).

13. See especially Jan Dumolyn, *Staatsvorming en vorstelijke ambtenaren in het graafschap Vlaanderen (1419-1477),* (Antwerp, 2003), pp. 200-09; Marc Boone, *Gent en de Bourgondische hertogen ca.1384- ca.1453: Een sociaal-politieke studie van een staatsvormingsproces* (Brussels, 1990); Marc Boone, *Geld en macht. De Gentse stadsfinanciën en de Bourgondische staatsvorming (1394-1453)* (Ghent, 1990). For an important study of the Bruges rebellion in 1436-8, see Jan Dumolyn, *De Brugse opstand van 1436-1438,* Standen en Landen, 101 (Kortrijk-Heule, 1997).

14. Blockmans and Donckers, 'Self-Representation', pp. 83-86; Élodie Lecuppre-Desjardin, 'Les lumières de la ville: recherche sur l'utilisation de la lumière dans les cérémonies bourgignonnes (XIVe-XVe siècles)', *Revue historique,* 301 (1999), pp. 23-43. I was unable to consult Élodie Lecuppre-Desjardin's new book (*La ville des cérémonies: espace public et communication symbolique dans les villes des Pays-Bas bourguinons (XIVe-XVe siècle),* (Turnhout, 2004) which appeared after this article was written.

zens in the aftermath of a rebellion.[15] As Peter Arnade writes, Burgundian state ceremony was constructed out of urban scaffolding.[16] Built from existing traditions, Burgundian ceremony also strengthened political authority through its power to play with the senses. It worked by virtue of its splendour: it dazzled its subjects (quite literally when bright light, from a ducal mansion or in a ceremonial Entry, flooded the civic landscape).[17] It involved them emotionally: 'collective emotions' generated though ritual cemented relations between ruler and ruled.[18] Evidently, this also was an indirect process. As Wim Blockmans and Esther Donckers hint, ritual deliberately sublimated the real differences between the two, and enclosed them in a wider symbolic union. Or as Arnade comments, ceremonies were not simple instruments of social control; they displaced conflict on to a ritual plane as a strategy to allow negotiation over political issues.[19]

These comments, however, raise more profound questions: how does ritual work and how does it relate to political power? The assumption that 'ritual generated political power'[20] requires more precise analysis. Arnade's remarks that ceremony should not be seen as external to the real workings of power or as a smoke-screen for that power, are partly based on a particular view of ritual, a view enshrined in an anthropological model famously offered by Clifford Geertz in his study of Negara.[21] Here, Geertz tells us, rulers who lacked political power, constructed a 'theatre-state' from a series of rituals which created a different form of power (an inner potency, radiating out from an exemplary centre) which held up, by reference to the supernatural order, idealized values in which both rulers and subjects could locate themselves.[22] This model has proved attractive to historians of the Burgundian Low Countries.[23] In both Bali and Burgundy, the presence of rituals could be related to the inadequacies of state power. Like the Balinese rulers, the dukes came to rule over a patchwork of territories which were difficult to control because of their disparate nature. Like the Balinese rulers, the dukes indulged in a large

15. Blockmans and Donckers, 'Self-Representation', pp. 87-90; Boone, 'La justice', 44.
16. Arnade, *Realms of Ritual,* p. 7.
17. *Ibid.,* pp. 26-7; Lecuppre-Desjardin, 'Lumières de la ville', 27-8.
18. Blockmans and Donckers, 'Self-Representation', pp. 82, 89, 91.
19. Ibid., pp. 110-11; Arnade, *Realms of Ritual,* pp. 211-13.
20. Blockmans and Donckers, 'Self-Representation', p. 89.
21. Arnade, *Realms of Ritual,* pp. 4-5
22. Clifford Geertz, *Negara. The Theatre-State in Nineteenth-Century Bali* (Princeton, 1981), esp. pp. 13-14, 102-5.
23. For the first application of the term to the Burgundian context, see Walter Prevenier and Wim Blockmans, *The Burgundian Netherlands* (Cambridge, 1986), p. 223.

range of spectacles: their Entry ceremonies, feasts and jousts are thus the Burgundian equivalents of Negaran ordinations, realm cleansings or tooth filings. Another analogy is that court spectacles in both Bali and Burgundy can be viewed as borrowing from local ones, which was partly why (in Geertz's Negara) subjects could recognize the ideals referred to and identify with their rulers.

The theatre-state model has also proved attractive because it apparently dovetails with the historiographical trend already discussed. Just as ducal power is seen as tending towards the destruction of urban liberties, so the Burgundian theatre-state is seen as functioning to assert, at a ceremonial level, ducal control over potentially rebellious subjects. There are slightly different versions of this theatre-state on offer, and how 'urban' or 'ducal' its ceremonies were;[24] but most imply some form of domination or appropriation of civic traditions by ducal authority. With reference to jousting, Évelyne van den Neste traces a development in which urban jousts such as the Epinette at Lille, were transformed from expressions of civic independence in the fourteenth century into symbols of civic subservience in the fifteenth, as the Burgundian dukes built up both their state and theatre-state.[25] As for the jousting events that the dukes organized themselves – the great *pas d'armes* which often took place within cities – these literally imposed courtly agenda on the city, veiling the civic landscape with theatrical props, scaffolding and sumptuous cloths. More generally, for Arnade, court ritual incorporated civic ritual: civic traditions in Ghent were not erased by the Valois dukes, but were made to serve ducal ends. Even so, the process was potentially a fraught one: since the relationship between ruler and ruled was essentially one of antagonism, ritual occasions involving duke and city rested on unstable foundations.[26]

24. David Nicholas sees the Burgundian theatre-state as neither Flemish nor urban ('In the Pit of the Burgundian Theater State: Urban Traditions and Princely Ambitions in Ghent 1360-1420', in *City and Spectacle in Medieval Europe,* ed. Barbara A. Hanawalt and Kathryn L. Reyerson, Minneapolis, 1994, p. 295); Arnade, however, sees it as fundamentally constructed out of 'urban scaffolding' (*Realms of Ritual,* p. 7). Both preserve a distinction between 'urban' and 'ducal', the one pitted against the other.

25. Évelyne van den Neste, *Tournois, joûtes, pas d'armes dans les villes de Flandre à la fin du Moyen Age (1300-1486)* (Paris, 1996), pp. 187-206 (esp. pp. 202-6 for 'la politique de l'état-spectacle'). Arnade seems to echo this subservience of local jousts to princely ones in his comment: 'Burgundian jousts in civic space represented a cultural hegemony [so] entrenched that it spawned imitative urban jousting companies' ('Urban Elites and the Politics of Public Culture in the Late-Medieval Low Countries', in *Hart en marge in de laat-middeleeuwse stedelijke maatschappij. Handelingen van het colloquium te Gent 1996,* eds. Myriam Carlier *et al.* (Leuven, 1997), p. 46).

26. Arnade, *Realms of Ritual,* p. 7.

   The application of Geertz's theatre-state to the Burgundian context, however, is problematic. Most historians who apply it suggest a clear and direct correlation between Burgundian ritual and Burgundian state-building. But Geertz was at pains to emphasize that in the Balinese theatre-state, ritual did not function as an adjunct of political power; the whole purpose of his book is to escape from the notion that somehow ritual is merely a mask disguising political power, the packaging that surrounds the real core of politics. The Negaran theatre-state purportedly creates a different kind of power (one based on an indigenous and non-Western concept) in which the court through its rituals becomes a microcosm of the heavenly order, while the realm through performance of state ritual comes to resemble the court and the heavenly order. The ritualized creation of the heavenly order was an end in itself, not a means to an end: 'power served pomp, not pomp power'. In almost all versions of the Burgundian theatre-state, however, pomp does serve power: ritual is highly functional, supporting the state-building efforts of the dukes, reflecting their growing political strength more often than their inadequacies.[27]

   A strict definition of Geertz's theatre-state is thus not usually applied to the Burgundian context. There are exceptions. Gordon Kipling's analysis of Entry ceremonies is closer to Geertz's original model and less interested in connections with state-formation. Duke and citizens perform their roles in 'microcosmal drama of the supernatural order'; by acting out the ideal political order they shape the 'imperfect world into an approximation of the supernatural order'.[28] In Kipling's Entry ceremonies, power does seem to serve pomp. Yet Kipling's 'purer' Geertzian approach raises a further set of problems. Critics of Geertz have pointed out that his theatre-state is not quite what it purports to be. In seeking to break down the distinction between 'ritual' and 'political action' (or expressive acts from instrumental action), Geertz nevertheless retains it in distinguishing 'pomp' from 'power'; and yet he has little to say about how ritual acts do in many cases become part of the normal political process, or how the exemplary centre of the Negaran court linked with the chaotic politics of the peripheries – which, according to other commentators in the same field, it undoubtedly did.[29] The Negaran theatre-state, despite what Geertz

   27. A point I have made more briefly before ('Bruges and the Burgundian "Theatre-State": Charles the Bold and Our Lady of the Snow', *History*, 84, 1999, 574-6).
   28. Gordon Kipling, *Enter the King. Theatre, Liturgy and Ritual in the Medieval Civic Triumph* (Oxford, 1998), esp. pp. 47, 50 note 4, 114.
   29. Stanley J. Tambiah, *Culture, Thought and Social Action. An Anthropological Perspective* (Harvard, 1985), pp. 316-38; James Laidlaw, 'On Theatre and Theory: Reflections on Ritual in Imperial Chinese Politics', in *State and Court Ritual in China*, ed. Joseph L. McDermott (Cambridge, 1999), pp. 399-416.

says to the contrary, may well have masked political power and hierarchy: how, after all, did the ideological underpinnings of the theatre-state (with its notion of power as an inner potency radiating from an exemplary centre to the peripheries) come to be established as the dominant discourse – except by the more mundane channels of hegemonic power exerted by Balinese rulers, the exercise of which is occluded in Geertz's analysis?[30]

In the end, Negaran pomp does indeed mask and serve power. Ironically, then, the Burgundian theatre-state, defined as a form of state power, is in fact close to its Balinese progenitor – not as Geertz defined it, but in what he denied it to be. This perhaps leaves the way open for the legitimate application of the term 'theatre-state' to the Burgundian context.[31] But it may, in the end, seem perverse to take up a model, defined so memorably in one way, and use it, without further clarification, to mean something contrary to what its original inventor intended.

The Ritual Process

The search for ritual models to explain the Burgundian context might in fact have taken other directions – away from Bali and towards mainland China. Certain studies of imperial China seem to offer models much closer to what is usually meant by the Burgundian theatre-state.[32] In China we can apparently find the imperial government, like the Burgundian one, actively intervening in local affairs and local traditions. Indeed, more strikingly analogous is the way in which the imperial court seems to have adopted certain local cults and converted them into symbols of imperial hegemony and state unity. Even better, recalling those cupidinous civic

30. Leo Howe, 'Rice, Ideology, and the Legitimation of Hierarchy in Bali', *Man: The Journal of the Royal Anthropological Institute,* (NS) 26 (1991), 445-67.

31. For a more self-conscious application of exactly this definition of the 'theatre-state', see Nicholas B. Dirks, *The Hollow Crown. Ethno History of an Indian Kingdom* (Cambridge, 1987), pp. 384-97, 401-4.

32. For the following see: James L. Watson, 'Standardizing the Gods. The Promotion of the T'ien Hou ("Empress of Heaven") Along the South China Coast, 960-1960', in *Popular Culture in Late Imperial China,* eds. David Johnson, Andrew J. Nathan and Evelyn S. Rawski (Berkeley, 1985), pp. 292-314; Prasenjit Duara, 'Superscribing Symbols: The Myth of Guandi, Chinese God of War', *Journal of Asian Studies,* 47:4 (1988), pp. 778-95; Paul S. Sangren, *History and Magical Power in a Chinese Community* (Stanford, 1987), pp. 215-25; Joseph McDermott, 'Emperor, Élites, and Commoners: the Community Pact Ritual of the Late Ming', in *State and Court Ritual in China,* ed. McDermott, esp. pp. 348-9; David Faure, 'The Emperor in the Village: Representing the State in South China', in *State and Court Ritual in China,* ed. McDermott, pp. 267-98.

officials complicit in Burgundian state-building, we discover in imperial China local elites anxious to promote imperial cults and interests in order to gentrify themselves.

My offer of an alternative model is, I confess, an empty gesture. The 'Chinese' model is appropriate only if we accept the various versions of the Burgundian theatre-state and how its rituals functioned at a local level. Most of these versions posit a fundamental antagonism between state and city underneath the surface of rituals in which duke and citizens were involved.[33] But princely engagement with civic rituals was not necessarily confrontational;[34] and as Graeme Small has shown, a more active model of exchange between 'court' and 'city', particularly in the construction of Entry ceremonies, needs to be incorporated into any formulation of a 'theatre-state'.[35] But the search for models may not be the most profitable approach to understanding ritual in the Burgundian context – especially if they merely confirm what the searcher is looking for. Models incorporate theories on how rituals are supposed to work, and these too are worth exploring.

Here again, assumptions made about certain kinds of Burgundian ritual are problematic. For instance, there are other difficulties with the Geertzian approach to ritual. The idea that somehow rituals can encapsulate the social order – so that the earthly order can become a microcosm of the heavenly – seems dangerously close (as Philippe Buc has pointed out) to a Durkheimian view that there is a natural and seamless correlation between the visions of the heavenly order and perceptions of the earthly; that religion is nothing more than an expression of society, and that religious rituals are the means to express it.[36] Moreover, to reduce 'rituals' to expressions of social order tells us little about how these rituals worked.[37]

In Durkheim's scheme of things, rituals work on participants because they present a vision of society at a sensory and emotional level. Rituals may indeed be effective because they discourage critical thinking: as

33. An argument put most memorably by Arnade, *Realms of Ritual,* pp. 5, 210-13.

34. Brown, 'Bruges and the Burgundian Theatre-State', 577-88.

35. Graeme Small, 'When *indiciaires* meet *rederijkers*: a Contribution to the History of the Burgundian "Theatre State"', in *Stad van koopmanschap en vrede. Literaire cultuur in Brugge op de grens van middeleeuwen en rederijkerstij,* ed. Jan Oosterman, Antwerpse studies over Nederlandse literatuurgeschiedenis, 12 (Leuven, 2005), pp. 133-161.

36. Philippe Buc, *The Dangers of Ritual. Between Early Medieval Texts and Social Scientific Theory* (Princeton, 2001), pp. 188-202.

37. Don Handelman, *Models and Mirrors. Towards an Anthropology of Public Events,* 2nd ed. (Oxford, 1999), pp. x-xliii.

David Kertzer writes, images of political ritual may be ambiguous in their meaning but direct in their emotional effect, and are made persuasive by stimulating the senses.[38] But to suggest that participants are changed by involvement in this world of symbols purely through having their 'collective emotions' stirred, is at best a dubious assumption. It risks relying on an anthropological tradition, predating even Durkheim, which tended to separate sensory emotion from rational thought, almost as though the participants who entered a ritual space left their reason at the threshold, to collect it again on their way out.[39] Some Burgundian ceremonies clearly required more cerebral attention than others. The complicated programme of Advent symbolism that Kipling has identified in Entry ceremonies as the means by which citizens hoped to transform the attitude of their ruler towards the city,[40] presumably demanded the agile engagement of the duke's cognitive faculties throughout.

Definition of 'ritual' is best left to anthropologists (amongst whom there is little agreement on the matter). But using some of their definitions allows more precision about how ritual is supposed to achieve things. Don Handelman, for instance, proposes an initial analysis of rituals detached from their social setting: by penetrating the logic of their design, we may better understand how different kinds of ritual are intended to work and how ultimately they relate to the social order. Rituals that are constructed as 'mirrors' (defined by Handelman as reflecting a version of the social order) work differently from those designed as 'models' (which present alternative worlds and reflect the existing social order much less).[41] The Burgundian Entry ceremony may be said to achieve its effect depending on what kind of design it is. If it were a 'mirror' kind of ritual, it would do so outside the event itself: the duke would presumably be left to reflect on the version of the social order that he had witnessed. If a 'model', the transformation on his faculties would be achieved within the event itself.[42]

38. David Kertzer, *Ritual, Politics and Power* (New Haven, Conn., 1988), p. 175.

39. Catherine Bell, *Ritual Theory, Ritual Practice* (Oxford, 1992), pp. 19-32.

40. Kipling, *Enter the King*, pp. 25-27; and for Philip the Good's Entry into Bruges in 1440, *ibid.*, pp. 49-60, 103-14.

41. Handelman, *Models and Mirrors*, esp. chapters 1 and 2.

42. Entry ceremonies would seem to conform to Handelman's pattern of modern pageants with historical processions, thus making them 'mirrors' (*Models and Mirrors*, pp. 41-8); but if emphasis is placed on Entries as 'liminal' events then they might be seen to act as 'models'. For the emphasis on liminality, see Jesse D. Hurlbut, 'Ceremonial Entries in Burgundy: Philip the Good and Charles the Bold, 1419-1477', Unpublished PhD thesis (Indiana State University, 1990). For Handelman's own qualifications to his scheme see *Models and Mirrors*, pp. 58-62.

It can be helpful to define what kind of ritual each ceremonial event is – although the nuances of an individual case (which the historian must consider) tend to defy anthropological modelling. But studies on the nature of rituals also alert us to the difficulties of establishing links between ritual and politics. To see ceremony as a 'cheaper' form of political control may be to assume a direct link between the two. Even in Geertz's theatre-state the way that ritualization can resolve social or political contradictions in the construction of some supernatural order is not a straightforward process. Much modern commentary on the nature of the ritual process goes further: it stresses how indirect and even indeterminate its effects are. Does it 'resolve' anything at all?

Ritual acts – to follow aspects of 'resistance' theory – may generate opposition as much as consent.[43] Even if treated as part of the dynamic of social empowerment, rather than as political control itself, ritual acts by their very performance may presuppose resistance towards the purpose of their agents. Geertz for instance does not comment on how willingly Balinese peasants complied with the theatre-state. The vision of the supernatural order presented in Burgundian Entries or processions may have had unintended effects. Given the monastic traditions of Christian thought which stressed the vanity of worldly things in contrast to the way of inner truth, the emphasis in sermons, homiletic literature and confessional tracts on the dangers and deceptions inherent in outer appearances, it may be doubted whether spectators of processions offering visions of heavenly order would ever have taken them at face value. If performances of ritual acts were inherently open to suspicion, rulers could not expect ritualized versions of their power to be accepted without question.

Ritual activity might also been seen as an act of gambling.[44] This is not merely because rituals might go wrong (as perhaps they threatened to do outside Bruges in 1457). It is also because they may even require unpredictability for them to work: the elements of play (or 'liminality' as some would prefer) inherent in the ritual process are perhaps essential generators of their transformative potential.[45] Furthermore, the symbols that rit-

---

43. On 'resistance theory' generally see James C. Scott, *Domination and the Art of Resistance: Hidden Transcripts* (New Haven, Conn., 1990); although for its limitations see for instance: Michael F. Brown, 'On Resisting Resistance', *American Anthropologist*, 98 (1996), pp. 729-35.

44. Buc, *Dangers of Ritual*, p. 8; Handelman, *Models and Mirrors*, pp. 63-81.

45. Perhaps we should not attempt to read a holistic programme into Entry ceremonies, as Kipling does: an unpredictable or even contradictory sequence of *tableaux* may be one mechanism which allows a particular ritual event to 'work' (see Handelman, *Models and Mirrors*, pp. 31, 63-81).

ual activity invoke make certainty of effect unlikely. If symbolic communication is defined as conveying a message in an indirect way, its meaning will evade immediate recognition, and remain obscure.[46] The shifting of a political problem onto a symbolic plane does not resolve the problem, but merely defers a solution without ever informing the participants directly what the earthly meaning of the supernatural order should be. Or (as other theorists would put it) the process casts them into a world of symbols which refer only to themselves; perhaps symbols are too indeterminate to allow fixed ideas to be imposed on them as forms of social or political control.[47] The difficulty of fixing the meaning of symbols used in processions was perhaps recognized by contemporaries: to instruct rulers on what they had seen during an Entry, city authorities began to produce books describing the event.[48] Alternatively, perhaps a ceremony works on participants, who may come to it with conflicting agenda, because they are made (or even deliberately choose) to 'misrecognize' what is going on: a holistic vision is maintained because different interpretations of it are allowed to stand and are not openly debated outside the ritual context.[49]

Some of this theorizing may seem to go too far. The logical extension of emphasizing the indeterminate nature of ritual is to argue that ritualized acts and symbols are so inherently unstable that they are capable of attracting an infinite number of interpretations and meanings. But to contemporaries these meanings might be finite, and the historian should try to define their parameters. One of the most promising lines of argument in present ideas of the Burgundian theatre-state has been the investigation into the relationship between princely rituals and urban ones, and how rulers engaged with the ceremonies they encountered in their towns.

46. See generally Gerd Althoff, 'Zur bedeutung symbolischer kommunikation für das verständnis des Mittelalters', *Frühmittelalterliche Studien,* 31 (1997), 370-389; Gerd Althoff and Ludwig Siep, 'Symbolische kommunikation und gesellschaftliche wertesysteme vom Mittelalter bis zur französischen Revolution. Der neue Münsterer Sonderforschungsbereich 496', *Frühmittelalterliche Studien,* 34 (2000), 413-446.

47. Bell, *Ritual Theory,* pp. 104-7, 204-18; Sangren, *History and Magical Power,* p. 4.

48. For the printed account of Charles V's Entry into Bruges in 1515, and earlier evidence for such books, see Blockmans and Donckers, 'Self-Representation', pp. 99-107 and especially Small, 'When *indiciaires* meet *rederijkers*'.

49. For a nice analogy – Escher's drawing of a flock of birds flying to the left that can be seen as a school of fish swimming to the right – see Sangren, *History and Magical Power,* p. 221.

It may be that the ritual acts or symbols used by dukes had the desired effect on citizens because they were already part of local rituals and meant something in their urban context. This is what Arnade or Blockmans in slightly different ways seem to imply. The dukes might be able to change the meaning of these acts and symbols to suit their purposes, but they had to start from a basis of familiarity. Their ceremonies had the power to move because they could be interpreted (even 'misrecognized') as local – rather than because they were 'splendid'.[50]

Let me return to the 'Chinese' model I was offering as an alternative to the 'Geertzian' theatre-state.[51] It is in fact rather unhelpful to current assumptions about Burgundian ritual. The imperial state in China did indeed incorporate local cults and rituals, and altered their meaning to suit its purposes, yet even when these were readopted at a local level, they remained open to reinterpretation by locals who did not necessarily see them as legitimating imperial control. State use of ritual was not fundamentally antagonistic towards local traditions; it could be subtle rather than crudely interventionist. But it was also a rather blunt instrument in asserting imperial hegemony, and was susceptible to redirection towards other purposes. The symbolic meanings of these rituals and cults were fixed enough for the state to make use of them and 'locals' to relate to them; but they remained ambiguous enough for 'locals' and for 'state officials' to choose and harmonize their own interpretations of them.

'Urban' and 'Princely' Ceremony in Bruges

Before some of these ideas can be applied to ceremonies in Bruges, clarification is required on how rulers related to them. The Holy Blood procession, the general processions and the jousts of the White Bear were all civic based and financed, and drew in the rulers of Flanders in particular ways. Involvement with these ceremonies inevitably required more circumspection than did indulgence in the great set-pieces of princely

50. See for instance Maurice Bloch, 'The Ritual of the Royal Bath in Madagascar: the Dissolution of Death, Birth and Fertility into Authority', in *Rituals of Royalty: Power and Ceremonial in Traditional Societies,* eds. David Cannadine and Simon Price (Cambridge, 1987), esp. p. 295. And for an emphasis on the need for organisers of rituals to refer to 'tradition', see Althoff, 'Zur bedeutung symbolischer kommunikation', pp. 386-87, and Jacoba van Leeuwen, *De Vlaamse wetsvernieuwing. Een onderzoek naar de jaarlijkse keuze en aanstelling van het stadsbestuur in Gent, Brugge en Ieper in de Middeleeuwen,* Verhandeling van de Koninklijke Vlaamse Academie van Belgie voor Wetenschappen en Kunsten, Nieuwe reeks (Brussels, 2004), pp. 255-58.

51. For references to the following, see above note 32.

magnificence, like the *pas d'armes*, meetings of the Order of the Golden
Fleece or banquets of the court. These urban ceremonies were also organized and paid for by the city – more specifically, by different (though
often overlapping) 'elite' groups within the city, who could also serve
sectional as well as 'civic' interests.

The Holy Blood procession seems to have emerged as a civic-wide
event by the late thirteenth century. From 1303 (or perhaps earlier) part
of the cortège began to carry the relic of the Holy Blood around the
perimeter of the new city walls which had been completed in 1297.[52] The
processional route thus enshrined an image of civic unity; its bringing
together, in the main procession, of different craft guilds and religious
institutions was intended to encapsulate a vision of civic harmony. A
desire for harmony may well have been sharpened in the wake of increasing internal tension within the city from the late thirteenth century, which
culminated after 1302 in the establishment of a new balance between the
different propertied groups and their representation in civic government.[53]
How exactly the event (and what parts of it) was financed in the early
fourteenth century – what the proportional balance was between expenditure laid out by guilds, religious houses and by the city itself – is
unclear. The city coffers contributed only a small amount to the procession even after 1303. But during the fourteenth century, the civic treasury
began to spend more on what looks like an increasingly elaborate event
– particularly after 1383 following the troubles during the Ghent war
which had seen popular disturbances (especially among the weavers)
within the city.[54] The regulation of a wider civic control over the sec-

52. It is a moot point as to whether the procession made a complete circuit of the walls
before 1303. The earliest reference to a Holy Blood procession to which guilds contributed
is in 1291 (the St John's bridgeloaders: E. Huys, *Duizend jaar mutualiteit bij de vlaamse
gulden* (Kortrijk, 1926), p. 150): the itinerary of the procession is unspecified. The first
mention of civic funding of the event is in 1303 (SAB, 216, 1303, fol. 24v) which refers
to the improvement of damp ground outside the city for the conveyance of the relic.
Expenses for bell ringing appear in the following year (SAB, 216, 1304, fol. 40r).
    53. For this interpretation see Thomas A. Boogaart II, *An Ethnogeography of Late
Medieval Bruges: Evolution of the Corporate Milieu, 1280-1349* (Lewisten, 2004), chapter 6. The involvement of craft guilds at this early stage is very plausible, although there
is no direct evidence – and no full description of the event exists until the sixteenth century. As for the new system of choosing the civic magistracy in 1304, and the extent of
craft guild involvement, there are difficulties of interpretation: see van Leeuwen, *De
Vlaamse wetsvernieuwing*, pp. 128-131.
    54. For brief comment on this, see Andrew Brown, 'Civic Ritual: the Counts of Flan-
ders and the City of Bruges in the Later Middle Ages', *English Historical Review,* 112
(1997), 283-4.

tional interests of craft guilds was no doubt further upheld and expressed in the annual procession. By the early fifteenth century, a new fraternity of the Holy Blood, apparently composed of former and senior city magistrates, also seems to have had increasing control over the procession and the relic housed in the chapel of St Basil.[55]

The annual jousting event was subject to similar changes.[56] The city treasury began regularly to fund the event from the 1320s, and with renewed vigour in the late fourteenth century after the Ghent war. It may then have undergone a change of name: in the 1370s it appears to have operated under the patronage of St George; in 1380 the leader of the jousts was for the first time referred to as 'the noble forester'; by 1391 at the latest, the jousts were called those of the 'White Bear'. The event does seem to have been regarded as a source of civic pride and wealth: as late as 1483, the city treasurers saw the expense as contributing to 'the honour of the town'. The jousters who took part represented a slightly different group of the 'civic elite' than the Holy Blood fraternity. Certainly, some of the known jousters were drawn from younger members of families who populated the two benches of city magistrates; a large proportion were from families of brokers, amongst the wealthiest merchants in Bruges, many but not all of whom entered city government. Others were from patricians with lordships or landed interests outside the city.

The organization and funding of 'general' or *ad hoc* processions involved another permutation of these and other groups in the city. The origins of such processions were certainly ecclesiastical: evidence for perambulations with relics to achieve peace and reconciliation is plentiful from at least the eleventh century; the provost of St Donatian in Bruges had paraded the relics of its patron saint on occasion to pacify the people.[57] This kind of procession may also have emerged as an extension

55. The existence of the fraternity is first mentioned in 1406 (SAB, 216, 1405-6, fol. 121v). Lists of members of the Holy Blood fraternity survive from 1469. Between 1469 and 1500, of the 73 names recorded, only six had not served on one of the city council's two benches (Archief van het Heilig-Bloed, Bruges, 18 (Rekeningen); SAB, 114, Wetsvernieuwingen 1468-1500). Entry into membership of the fraternity seems to have followed a period in civic office.

56. For the following see Andrew Brown, 'Urban Jousts in the Later Middle Ages: The White Bear of Bruges', *Revue Belge de Philologie et d'Histoire*, 78 (2000), 315-30, and Andries van den Abeele, *Het Ridderlijk Gezelschap van de Witte Beer* (Bruges, 2000).

57. Galbert of Bruges, *The Murder of Charles the Good*, ed. James B. Ross (New York 1959; repr. Toronto, 1967), pp. 44, 163. For a procession of the relics of Saints Donatian, Basil and Maximus to meet the corpse of the murdered count (1127), see *ibid.*, p. 246. For suggestive comments about the beginnings and functions of general processions, see Jacques Chiffoleau, 'Les processions parisiennes de 1412. Analyse d'un rituel flamboyant', *Revue historique*, 114 (1990), 37-76.

of the liturgical traditions associated with Rogation.[58] The propitiatory function of these processions of relics is often referred to in St Donatian's chapter act-books (extant from 1345): amongst their purposes are listed the prevention of plague or bad weather and the hope for good harvests, for the 'serenity of the airs', and for peace.[59] The chapter act-books also show that an increasing number of these processions was undertaken in the fifteenth century (and especially from the 1450s), and that the relics most used were those from the church itself – particularly those of St Donatian and St Basil.[60] Some of these processions were organized on the initiative of the collegiate church itself:[61] indeed the college at times insisted on its right to be the chief organizer of these events, above the other main churches in Bruges.[62] But quite evident too is that a majority of these processions set out at the request of the town magistrates – whose own accounts mention payments towards a 'general procession' for the first time in September 1408.[63]

These, then, were the groups of citizens and clergy with which the rulers of Flanders had to engage when making use of ceremonial traditions within Bruges. Make use of them they did – especially from the late fourteenth century. The Valois dukes attended the jousting event with increasing frequency from the 1390s, even more so from the 1440s.[64] In some ways though their involvement had been prefigured by their Dampierre predecessors in Flanders: Louis de Male attended the event in 1353, no doubt as part of an effort to curry favour in Flanders for his wider dynastic ambition to secure the duchy of Brabant. In other ways the involvement of the Burgundian dukes was surpassed by that of their Hapsburg successor in the crisis years following the death of Charles the Bold. The highest expenditure on civic jousts occurred under Maximil-

58. In 1382 (one of the earliest reference to such processions in St Donatian's fabric accounts) the relics of St Donatian and St Basil were taken out, on two separate occasions, apparently in response to an earthquake: the destination of St Basil was to three religious houses, on the outskirts of the town, which were also the destinations of annual processions at Rogation (BAB, G2, fols. 9r-9v). For Rogation processions to the churches of Mary Magdalen, St Catherine and St Cross, see for instance, BAB, A48, fol. 88v (1381); A50, fol. 66v (1419).

59. For the earliest references in the *Acta Capituli*, see BAB, A50, fols. 91v, (August 1420); 125v (June 1422); fol. 226 (July 1435).

60. For figures on relics, see Brown, 'Civic Ritual', 290 note 1. For number of processions see figures below, note 67.

61. This seems to be the case particularly up to the 1450s; thereafter the ones organized on the initiative of the college itself, or taking place within the church, seem to be referred to as 'processiones particulares' or 'privatas' (e.g. BAB, A52, fol. 93v (February 1459); A53, fol. 68 (April 1464).

62. The claim occurs in a case over the rights of burial pertaining to the church (BAB, I13).

63. SAB, 216, 1408/9, fol. 85v.

ian in 1479 and 1481 when his presence in the city was intended to encourage acceptance of his rule.

Princely use of general processions was also mounting in the fifteenth century. It may be that even the early requests and payments by the town magistrates for processions had been at princely behest: the procession in September 1408 had been for the 'victory of the prince against the rebels of Flanders' (the Liègeois); a sermon was preached by a friar in December 1411 for Duke John's welfare in Paris, and another in July 1412, this time on a general procession to the Eekhout abbey in Bruges; the mendicant orders of the town were paid in March 1414, as part of the processions to the beguinage and other churches, for fourteen sermons preached for the duke's welfare on his journey to Paris.[65] The increasing number of these processions from the 1450s may also have come from princely initiative – though if so, princely requests to St Donatian for use of its relics seem to have been made indirectly through the town magistrates rather than directly to the collegiate church or through the count's officials (the *schout* and *baljuw*) in Bruges.[66] In the 1460s the number of processions intensified;[67] but they reached a height in the crisis years,

64. For the following see Brown, 'Urban Jousts', 315-30 and Abeele, *Ridderlijk Gezelschap*.

65. SAB, 216: 1408/9, fol. 85v; 1411/12, fols. 92v, 97v; 1413/14, fols. 86, 90. For Burgundian involvement in processions in Paris around the same date, see Chiffoleau, 'Les processions parisiennes de 1412', 48, 68-70. For John the Fearless's efforts to increase ducal control over the system of choosing the magistracy in this period, see van Leeuwen, *De Vlaamse wetsvernieuwing*, pp. 153-57.

66. The *Acta Capituli* usually record that the request for a procession came from the civic authorities; though on 12 July 1474, they record additionally that the 'scabini' of Bruges had received letters from the duke of Burgundy asking for three general processions to be held on successive days (BAB, A54, fol. 45).

67. The number of processions in any one year is difficult to reconstruct because the sources in which they are referred to are multiple, sometimes contradictory, and not complete. Occasionally (in the church of St Donatian) daily or weekly processions were ordered for an indefinite period, making calculation of an exact total of processions impossible. The two main (continuous) sources are the town accounts (SAB 216), the St Donatian *Acta Capituli* (BAB A50-A57), supplemented by the (incomplete) St Donatian Fabric Accounts (BAB G2-G7). Chronicles provide more information for the later fifteenth century (from the 1460s: HS 436 and HS 437; from 1478: *Het boeck van al 't gene datter geschiet es binnen Brugge sichent Jaer 1477, 14 Februarii, tot 1491*, ed. C. Carton (Ghent, 1859) *passim*); from the 1490s see: SAB, 120, Hallegeboden). For the ones involving the Holy Blood (after 1469): Archief van het Heiligbloed, H. Bloedbasiliek, Bruges, 18. But even this list does not exhaust the range of sources I have used for the figures shown below. I hope to publish a fuller account of general processions elsewhere. For now the average number of general processions (per decade, with the peak year in each decade shown) during the fifteenth century is as follows: 1400s: 0 (1 in 1408); 1410s: 1; 1420s: 2; 1430s 3 (7 in 1436); 1440s: 4; 1450s: 6 (13 from October 1457 to September 1458); 1460s: 10 (16 in 1468); 1470s: 15 (28 in 1474); 1480s: 18 (28 in 1482); 1490s: 8 (13 in 1490).

under Maximilian, during the 1480s – an intensity also apparent in the increasing use of sermons[68] and multiple combinations of relics during a single procession.[69] There were other novelties under Maximilian. Processional routes of these relics seem to have followed time-honoured routes: certain relics had their own *via sacra*.[70] But unusually on two occasions in 1478, general processions were guided round the *prinsenhof* (the princely residence) in Bruges,[71] as though the centre of princely power within the city was by then exerting a stronger gravitational pull on relics in Bruges.

The Holy Blood relic was subject to the same forces of princely authority. Charles the Bold's attendance at the annual procession of 3 May in 1457 was not unusual. The counts of Flanders had been represented at the procession by their officials, the *baljuw* and *schout* from at least the 1330s;[72] but the counts themselves could attend the event – as Count Louis did in 1382, no doubt as part of his effort to drum up support for his war against Ghent.[73] But Charles's request in 1465 for the Holy Blood to be used on a general procession was in fact a novel use of the relic: for the first time it was taken out of its chapel on an occasion other than the annual event in May and transported to a city church (that of Our Lady). In the 1470s Charles subjected the relic to further perambulation on five more occasions; but his successors expected the relic to be more energetic still. Between 1477 and 1488 it received its marching orders on fifteen occasions (in 1479 on four separate days).[74] There were other novelties. Whereas Charles had been content in 1457 to watch the Holy Blood

68. A peak seems to have occurred in 1485 when 159 sermons were preached from February to May (SAB, 216, 1484/5).

69. This phenomenon is harder to document because the town accounts (on which we are reliant up until the 1460s) do not always tell us which relics were transported; while the references to processions in the St Donatian *Acta Capituli* for the same period are sparser. But it seems that from 1471, processions in which more than one relic was transported became more frequent. The combination favoured was the 'drie riven', the principal relics from each of the three main parish churches in Bruges (St Donatian, Our Lady, St Saviour) – as on 4 April 1471 (HS 437, fols. 350r-50v). The carrying of St Donatian's relics with relics from other churches was not always approved of by the clergy of St Donatian, and their complaints at this practice also increase from the 1470s (see below).

70. The favoured routes of particular relics can be traced from the following sources: HS 437; *Het boeck,* ed. Carton; and SAB, 120, Hallegeboden. I hope to look at these *via sacra* in more detail elsewhere.

71. HS 437, fols. 413r-13v (8 May), 418r (24 June). The second occasion was in thanksgiving for the birth of Mary of Burgundy's son Philip.

72. Payments to them for gloves (for carrying torches) can be found by the 1330s; by 1350 they were being paid a regular sum of 18 *livres* at the event (SAB, 216, 1349/50, fol. 118v).

73. HS 436, fol. 148.

74. For sources for these figures see above, note 67.

pass by from his platform, Maximilian actually inserted himself into the procession itself. On 8 September 1477 he and his wife walked behind the Holy Blood to 'ask the grace of God against his enemy';[75] and when news came to Bruges that Maximilian had been successful against Louis XI at Guinegate in August 1479, his wife walked barefoot behind the relic, accompanied by torches with arms of the town and those of the Holy Blood fraternity, by way of thanksgiving.[76] To pray for her husband's success, she had already asked on 17 May of that year for the relic to be taken to the hospital of Mary Magdalen – outside the town walls, further than the relic had ever travelled on a general procession before.[77]

Such changes in the use of relics might well suggest a growing princely appropriation of local traditions. But there are two qualifications to make. The implication that there is a clear difference between 'princely' and 'local' traditions should be resisted; so should the notion that we are witnessing a process by which a 'foreign' dynasty imposed its rule on a 'native' population. The relics put to such exertions were not 'civic' in origin. The body of St Donatian had been the gift of Count Baldwin of Flanders to the collegiate church about 862 – as the college reminded Philip the Good around 1464.[78] Similarly the relics of St Basil had been the gift of Count Philip of Alsace in 1186, memory of which was also recalled by the clergy of St Donatian when Philip the Good attended a lavish translation ceremony of the reliquary of St Basil in 1463.[79] In any case the collegiate church had special and ancient connections with the duke and his household: its provost was selected by the count; the church had originally formed part of the count of Flanders' castle; and it had claims to be the chief burial place in the town for the count and his household officers – a legal claim that the church was keen to impress on Duke

75. HS 437, fol. 398v. On 6 August 1486 Maximilian inserted himself next to the Holy Blood on another general procession of the relic (*Het boeck,* ed. Carton, pp. 131-2).

76. *Het boeck,* ed. Carton, p.16.

77. *Het boeck,* ed. Carton, p. 12. On March 27, with Mary on her deathbed, the Holy Blood and the body of St Donatian (a rare combination of relics) was processed once again outside the city gates to the Carthusian priory (BAB, A55, fol. 162v; *Het boeck,* ed. Carton, p. 37).

78. BAB, I13 contains bundles of documents to do with the litigation over the burial rights of St Donatian. Some of the litigation came before the council of the duke. One of the rolls is described as a 'memoire' concerning the history of the church, and dates the arrival of the relic of St Donatian to Bruges to 862. But for a dating of 864, see P. Grierson, 'The Translation of the Relics of Saint Donatian to Bruges', *Revue Bénédictine,* 49 (1937), 170-90.

79. BAB, A52, fol. 246v.

Philip the Good in 1463.[80] Within the count's castle the chapel of St Basil
had also been built by Count Diederic in the mid-twelfth century (and
rebuilt by Count Philip of Alsace after a fire in 1187). Quite when it
acquired the relic of the Holy Blood is uncertain; but by the fourteenth
century a tradition existed that it was the gift of Count Diederic in the
twelfth century.[81] Thus Burgundian use of these relics should not be perceived simply as an 'appropriation' of 'civic' ceremonies. The traditions
of the counts of Flanders were embedded in local urban traditions: the
dukes of Burgundy did no more than latch on to cults to which they, as
counts of Flanders, were legitimate heirs.

Burgundian and Hapsburg use of the Holy Blood relic on general processions was more of a 'reappropriation'. Since the relic had become
anchored to civic ceremony by the later thirteenth century, princely call
on it meant a reassertion of its original comital connections. But even
this use did not break with civic traditions associated with the relic.
Charles the Bold's request in 1465 was connected with his hostile ven-
tures against the French; as was subsequent use of the relic by Charles
and by his Hapsburg successor. Maximilian's victory over the French in
August 1479 (which had involved the Bruges civic militia) was celebrated
by another procession of the Holy Blood, and by bringing the standard
of Bruges back to St Basil's chapel to be placed before the relic.[82]

While such use of the Holy Blood served new dynastic purposes, it
was done so in a way that perhaps showed an awareness of civic traditions connected with the relic. Resistance to French sovereignty had been
one of the contexts out of which the Holy Blood procession had originally
emerged. In September 1297, the threat posed to Flanders by the armies
of King Philip the Fair had led the magistrates of Bruges to seek assur-
ance that the king would leave their Holy Blood relic where it was.[83] The
new walls around Bruges, completed in 1297, were soon under threat:
early in 1302 the French governor of Flanders was on the point of dis-
mantling the ramparts when a mob led by the weaver Pieter de Coninck
put a stop to his efforts. On 17 May, a small French force entered the
city and was ambushed and massacred (the *Brugse Metten*); the gover-

80. BAB, I13.
81. N. Huyghebaert, 'Iperius et la translation de la relique du Saint Sang à Bruges',
Annales de la Société d'émulation de Bruges, 100 (1963), 110-87. The earliest documented
reference to the relic in Bruges is in 1256.
82. *Het boeck,* ed. Carton, pp. 15-16; SAB 216: 1478/9, fols. 174r, 174v, 177r, 178v;
1479/80, fol. 150v.
83. SAB 96, 2 (Rodenboek), fols. 29r-29v. For later French atrocities against Flemish
relics in May 1302 (the beheading of images 'as if they were alive'), see *Annales Gan-
denses,* ed. Hilda Johnstone (Oxford, 1985), p. 28.

nor was forced to flee, and declared the city forfeit of its liberties. The large French army sent to pacify Flanders was famously defeated by the Flemish urban militia at Kortrijk in July. The following year, in May 1303, the city first began to make payments towards guarding the relic and towards improving the route outside the city gates which made possible (or easier) a complete circuit of the city walls.[84] Over the next few years, the chapel of St Basil and the reliquary which contained the Holy Blood were refurbished at the city's expense, official approval from the bishop of Tournai was sought, and a papal bull was acquired (at the customary vast expense) from Clement V. The bull offered indulgences to those who visited the relic, which was now credited with miraculous powers of liquefaction. While this new investment must be set in the context of changes in civic government that also followed the events of the *Metten*,[85] it must also be set within a period when the walls of the city had been delivered from destruction by French royal authority. Such a connection was made later – though in a context hostile to Bruges: in 1348 a pro-French chronicler at Tournai, at the abbey of St Martin, claimed that the Holy Blood relic had in fact ceased to liquefy because of the treachery of the Bruges citizens against the French governor in 1302.[86] A possible association of the Holy Blood with hostility to the French may have been precisely what Charles the Bold had hoped to resurrect in 1465.

The manner in which the relic was used suggests something further about princely 'appropriation' of civic ceremony: it had to work with, rather than against, the grain of local traditions. The use made by the Burgundian dukes of general processions could also be presented as traditional rather than novel or inappropriate. The earliest mention of payment for a procession in St Donatian's fabric accounts was in 1381 – following news of Count Louis de Male's victory against Ghent at Nevele.[87]

84. Certainly a sense of civic responsibility for the upkeep of the route only begins in 1303 (see above note 52). For continued improvements to the processional route outside the city see: SAB, 216, 1306, fol. 10.

85. Boogaart, *Ethnogeography of Late Medieval Bruges*, chapter 6.

86. Gilles li Muisis, *Chronique,* ed. H. Lemaitre (Paris, 1905), p. 65. The implications for relations between the city and bishop of Tournai concerning the Holy Blood also need assessing more fully. For instance, Bruges seems to have stopped sending representatives to the annual procession of Our Lady in Tournai in the early fourteenth century, just at the time when the Holy Blood procession was becoming established as a civic event. For the importance of episcopal confirmation of the procession before 1311, see Alfons Dewitte, 'Ons Heren Bloet, 1311', *Biekorf,* 103 (2003), 187-8.

87. BAB, G2, 1380/1, fol. 55v. In 1382 following the count's victory at Rosebeke, there was also a 'procession with torches' to the Markt amidst scenes of 'great joy' (HS

The earliest reference in the chapter act-books of St Donatian declare that the purposes of general processions were 'for good weather, for peace,' and – it is added – 'for the prince'.[88]

It was as natural for the dukes of Burgundy to make use of the jousts in Bruges. The name of the event (White Bear) and its leader (the 'forester'), names adopted from perhaps 1380 onwards, had been chosen with comital traditions in mind. Chronicles of Flanders had long traced the origins of the county back to Liederic de Buc who had reputedly acquired the title of 'forester' in the seventh century; they also credited the first count, Baldwin 'Iron Arm' (867-97), with the feat of clearing Flemish forests of polar bears.[89] Count Louis de Male had been fully apprised of his heroic ancestors, and had perhaps been intent on encouraging memory of them within Flanders: by 1374 he had images of his predecessors, back to Liederic, painted full length (with inscriptions in Middle Dutch) on the walls of his chapel at Kortrijk.[90] Perhaps the new name of the Bruges jousts had been chosen by a group favourably inclined to the count in the context of his war against Ghent. As successors to the Dampierre counts of Flanders, the dukes of Burgundy found in these jousts associations which suited their interests and allowed their involvement in them to be perceived as 'traditional'.

The need to work with the grain of 'civic traditions', however, also placed limitations on the use by rulers of urban ceremony. By no means all the associations generated by ceremonial events could be turned to princely advantage. Engagement with the Holy Blood procession did not mean the straightforward harnessing of a source of anti-French feeling or even of a force for collective unity. Local chronicles make no explicit link between resistance to the French and the origins of the procession; and they would have had no reason to link citizen resistance in the early fourteenth century with the count of Flanders who had then been in no position to defy the king of France. Moreover, united opposition to French sovereignty in the 1290s and 1300s had been absent in Bruges. The city's ruling elite had been evenly divided between those who ostensibly supported the Flemish count (the 'Claws') and those who supported the

436, fols. 149v-50r). The fabric accounts do not refer to this, but for the motet 'Comes Flandriae' composed for the occasion, see Reinhard Strohm, *Music in Late Medieval Bruges* (Oxford, 1990), p. 104.

88. BAB, A50, fols. 91v (1420), 125v (1422), 244v (1437).

89. For references see Brown, 'Urban Jousts', 315-30 and Abeele, *Ridderlijk Gezelschap*.

90. F. Vandeputte, 'La chapelle des contes de Flandre à Courtrai', *Annales de la société d'emulation de Bruges*, 10 (1875), 189-212; and Vale, *The Princely Court*, p. 230.

French king (the 'Lilies'); only in 1302 had a 'Claw' magistracy been installed. There were also other divisions among the propertied classes which were to culminate in the restructuring of civic office-holders after 1302, allowing the participation of a broader segment of propertied groups.[91] The Holy Blood procession had thus become a civic event in a climate of faction, disunity and discontent; linking the city and its guilds with the cosmic order, it was less a celebration of civic independence as the expression of a desire for stability which the propertied no doubt wished to see restored.

Moreover, the annual assertion of the city's hierarchy and place in the cosmic scheme of things was no guarantee of social order. The disruption during the period of the Ghent war (1379-83) had involved radical elements within Bruges, especially the weavers, clashing with civic authorities. It had also seen disruption to the Holy Blood procession, for less was spent on the event during the war. The return of peace seems to have led to the elaboration of the procession, perhaps as a reassertion of hierarchy: from 1389 an increasing amount was spent by the civic authorities on more musicians, torches, new *tableaux vivants* and the wider involvement of the city's clergy in the procession.[92] It was probably in this period that the fraternity of the Holy Blood, exclusive to senior aldermen, assumed greater control over the event and the relic.

Participants in the procession perhaps read their own meaning into the event. It was an occasion when sectional interests might further their own agenda. The college of St Donatian used it as an opportunity to assert its claim to preeminence over the monks of Eekhout abbey (an issue of long-standing grievance): in 1500 it led to an assault by one of the monks on one of the canons during the procession itself.[93] Craft guilds could use Holy Blood day to affirm their own economic privileges. The barber-surgeons in 1423 chose the day as the occasion to assert superiority over the equivalent guild in the port of Sluis: every year on that day the Sluis guild was to hand over four pipes of wine to the barber-surgeons of Bruges.[94] It was also an occasion when other agenda could be asserted.

91. Boogaart, *Ethnogeography of Late Medieval Bruges*, chapter 6.

92. For references, see Brown, 'Civic Ritual', pp. 283-5. For disruption to the system of choosing the civic magistracy during this period see van Leeuwen, *De Vlaamse wetsvernieuwing*, pp. 137-42.

93. BAB: A57, fol. 144v, 225v; I12; SAB 96, 113 (Groenenboek C), fols. 317v-19. I hope to comment in more detail on this case in a later publication.

94. RAB, Fonds blauw nummers, 8120. For similar demands by other guilds in Bruges, see the chandlers in 1424 (RAB bl.numm. 8122) and in 1450 (ibid., 8194); the weavers in 1456 (ibid., 8183); and the coopers in 1458: (SAB, 336, Cupers inschrijvingsregister, fol. 94v).

In 1475, one Regnault Willems chose 3 May on which to express his irritation at being forced to become dean of the plumbers' guild: he deliberately appeared in the procession, at the place appointed for his guild, without the regulation yellow sash around his shoulder. His sartorial defiance had apparently generated more dangerous unrest according to the civic magistracy: among the members of the guild, who were gathered there in great number, discontented mutterings had begun. So serious had the threat to civic order been, that the city magistrates had pronounced Willems banished from Flanders for fifty years.[95] The staging of the procession itself, with so many groups of citizens involved, had become a potential threat to civic peace. Its use as an instrument of princely authority was not necessarily an assured support for stable rule.

Saddling up at the Bruges jousts was also not certain to further princely power. The event might be perceived as a source of civic pride, but it could also be identified as a seat of sectional interest. In times of crisis, when more radical elements within the city were in rebellion, the event did not take place. During the troubles of the Ghent war, virtually no jousts were funded by the city treasury: the renewal of the event, with its new name of the White Bear, was perhaps part of a wider reassertion of 'patrician' control within the city, of which vigorous funding of ceremony of all kinds, including the Holy Blood procession, was also a part.[96] Similarly, during the rebellion against Duke Philip the Good in 1436-8, 'no aristocratic games', according to one Bruges chronicler, were held in 1437.[97] In times of crisis, reliance on the ties forged with this particular group of the civic elite did not promote ducal control over the city as a whole. Among the citizens loyal to Duke Philip was a 'forester' of the White Bear, Morisis van Varsenare: he was killed by rebels specifically 'because he worked with the prince to keep down the common people of Bruges'. During the upheaval of rebellion against Maximilian in the 1480s, the White Bear jousters were also regarded as a faction too supportive of princely interests. The execution in 1488 of Arnoud Breydel, former 'forester' and excluded from civic office early that year (after a radical government had imprisoned Maximilian within the city) was a result of his support of the prince. No further civic funds were ever spent on the White Bear jousts. As the tool of faction, the White Bear jousts could not always serve as an instrument of state control.

95. HS 437, fols. 364r-64v; SAB 157 (Civiele Sententiën Vierschaar), fols. 144v-47. I intend to comment on this case in more detail in a later publication.
96. For references to the following, see Brown, 'Urban Jousts', 323-24, 326-27, 330.
97. HS 436, fol. 190.

Manipulation of general processions for princely purposes was also not assured. If the 'welfare of the prince' was regarded as one of the appropriate functions of these processions, interpretations might differ as to how this welfare might be best secured. In times of crisis, peace mattered as much as princely victory. Processions arranged for the duke during war often coupled prayers for the prince with prayers for peace. The Holy Blood relic was processed to St Donatian's on 19 May 1475 partly to support Duke Charles in the field against his enemies at Neuss, but also to further the peace-seeking efforts of the papal legate who was also present there.[98] The Holy Blood did not set off only when the French were being fought: in 1488, 1490 and 1491 it also ventured out of its chapel in processions to celebrate or pray for peace.[99] Charles himself seems to have recognized that expressing a desire for peace would play better with his urban subjects than proclaiming his wish for military victory: in 1475 he issued instructions for his towns to conduct processions on his behalf to persuade citizens of his 'great desire for peace'.[100] The reason most frequently given for processions in chronicles and chapter act-books of St Donatian (particularly in the crisis years from 1477 to 1492) was the need for peace, outside and within the city.[101]

What the chapter act-books also record is a perception of processions and relics that could be resistant to both princely and civic command. Ultimately, the relics of St Donatian's belonged to the church. For the collegiate clergy, St Donatian, 'our patron', was principally the 'author of peace'; so was St Basil.[102] The clergy had been prepared to allow the growing number of requests from the 1460s for these relics to be used in general processions; but they were not always content to bow to secular demands. On 8 June 1467 they were already grumbling that 'ancient customs' were being violated in the latest request from the civic magistrates for processions.[103] Over the next decade, and especially during the 1480s

98. HS 437, fol. 362v.
99. *Het boeck,* ed. Carton, pp. 223, 385, 437.
100. Quoted in Gilliodts-van Severen, *Inventaire des archives de la ville de Bruges* (Bruges, 1871-85), VI, p. 108.
101. Of the 83 processions for which explicit motive is given (in the *Acta Capituli* and chronicles) between 1420 and 1492, 60 include 'peace' as a purpose. Most of the rest were to ward off pestilence or bad weather; a handful were to celebrate the more peaceful princely successes – marriage and birth of heirs.
102. For references to St Donatian and St Basil as 'auctores pacis', see for instance BAB, A55, fol. 29 (1484); A56, fol. 205 (1489).
103. BAB, A53, fol. 231v. The complaint on this occasion was also against the 'interference' of the bishop of Tournai's representative in Bruges (the 'dean of Christianity'). The long-standing quarrels over jurisdiction between St Donatian's and the bishop of Tournai adds a further dimension to the issue.

when the call on their relics was at its peak, confrontations increased with the civic authorities. On five occasions in the 1480s, the college refused to allow the relics of its patron saint to be processed.[104] In May 1485, dispute seems to have been acrimonious. Deputies shuttled back and forth between collegiate chapter and civic chambers. The canons let it be known that great denigration and harm had been done to the church's patron saint; that his body was on no account to be processed at the same time as relics from other churches, and only on occasions of 'greatest necessity' and with a veneration commensurate with St Donatian's ancient status.[105]

Conclusion

The forester Liederic de Buc, the body of St Donation and the relic of the Holy Blood all appeared together on the same street in Bruges in 1515 – or rather representations of them did. They formed part of the first three *tableaux vivants* that greeted the young Charles V as he entered the city for the first time.[106] They also formed part of a series of *tableaux* – interrupted by several staged by the foreign merchants of Bruges – which the civic authorities evidently hoped would stir Charles (or his advisors) into action to arrest the decline of the city. Their *tableaux* illustrated chronologically the historical links between Bruges and the counts of Flanders, culminating in a representation of Charles himself with his hand poised on the Wheel of Fortune. The earthly message of the Entry (for once) seems clear enough, although quite how Charles reacted to it is not known. Certainly he was entertained, asking for the event to be set up again on the following day. Perhaps, like the dauphin Louis fifty years previously, he was more struck by the pageants put on by the foreign merchants – and was literally so, when the gunpowder-filled tower restaged by the Aragonese blew up in his face. His horse had reared, his aunt Margaret of Austria had been showered with sparks, and terrified crowds had surged around him. No lasting harm was done to

104. BAB, A55, fols. 212r (May 1483); A56, fols. 46r (August 1484), 71v-72r (May 1485), 73r (May 1485), 95r (February 1486). The first occasion when the collegiate clergy seem to have refused to allow the relics of St Donatian be carried in procession was in August 1473 (BAB, A54, fol. 48).
105. BAB, A56, fols. 71v-72r.
106. For the following, see Remi de Puys, *La tryumphante entree de Charles prince des Espagnes en Bruges 1515*, ed. Sydney Anglo (Amsterdam, 1973), *passim*.

relations between prince and city; but the Entry seems to have done no lasting good. Charles did little to prevent the city's decline. This despite the illustrated book of the Entry that the city quickly produced and dispatched to the court (and for wider circulation) to ram the message home. Perhaps the meaning of the whole event had not been as clear as the civic authorities had intended: certainly comment made in the text on some of the pageants put on by foreign merchants betray a concern that these were out of step (again!) with the civic agenda.

Symbolic communication between prince and city had never been straightforward. The staging of it always involved risk. Large spectacles involving crowds were inherently risky. Meanings of messages were always open to alternative interpretations or 'misrecognition'. The second *tableau* in the 1515 Entry, representing the gift of Count Baldwin to Bruges of the relic of St Donatian, could be interpreted in several ways: as encouragement for continued generosity of count to city (as the Bruges' authorities might have intended); as justification for princely exploitation of civic relics (as Burgundians and Hapsburgs had done in general processions); or as an appeal to the rights of custodianship over these relics of the clergy of St Donatian – who are shown as the reliquary's recipients. These were ambiguous and unstable foundations for the 'imposition' of any 'theatre state.'

The term 'Burgundian theatre-state', however, needs revision, perhaps abandonment, as a useful description of princely ceremony. If it is to float as a meaningful concept, it needs to be deliberately cut loose from its Geertzian moorings. But if the term is supposed to imply the imposition of state power by ceremonial means, it quickly begins to flounder. Princes could not simply impose political authority through rituals. Civic authorities, and groups within the city, stamped their own meaning on ceremonial events, especially if they paid for them. The splendour or frequency of princely ceremonies did not always correlate directly to the strength of state power. Ironically, the period in which rulers had most recourse to the relics, general processions and jousts of Bruges was in the late 1470s and 1480s – when Burgundian and Hapsburg power was most under threat. In any case, 'imposition' is too strong a word for a ritual process that required careful engagement with urban traditions. It also implies a fundamental distinction and antagonism between 'urban' and 'princely' traditions. But the distinction should not be overdrawn. In the first place, some of these traditions were not 'civic' at all. In its use of relic processions Burgundian 'state-ceremony' was constructed out of scaffolding that was ecclesiastical rather than princely or civic. And the relic of St Donatian, as the canons implied in 1485, answered to the church's own needs: it could not be incorporated without friction into the rituals of state or city. Secondly, princely and civic traditions were not mutually exclusive. In their use of processions, particularly with relics of the Holy Blood or St Donatian, state authorities called on ceremonial forms in which comital and urban traditions were entangled with one another. It was this entanglement that made such use of ceremonies possible but restricted.

The University of Edinburgh

Christoph Friedrich WEBER

PUBLIC ENCOUNTERS BETWEEN THE CITY COUNCIL
AND THE EPISCOPAL LORD IN LATE MEDIEVAL BASEL:
ROUTINE JOBS OR TRANSITIONS
IN SYMBOLIC COMMUNICATION?[1]

By taking up a current discussion, the introduction to the conference held in Leuven 2003 has encouraged us to look at the late medieval town from the perspective of symbolic communication. Although having been applied thoroughly on the early and high Middle Ages, this research paradigm still provides a chance for historians to face the diversity of late medieval sources.[2] The relation between tradition and innovation, the flexibility of participants and spectators, or the open structures of civic rituals are addressed here. Additionally, we have to consider the hermeneutic dimension hinted at in the introduction: when can a ritual be considered as understood, and if it is understood, is it also successful?

To my mind, public encounters are highly suitable for an investigation in this sense.[3] As the status of the participants was generally certain, the encounters of the rulers and the ruled displayed the allocation of roles within medieval relations of power. Given the assumption that symbolic communication belonged to the 'cold' surface of medieval societies,[4] one will note, that even seemingly spontaneous behaviour of people in late medieval times, who were considered as worthy enough to appear as

1. In consideration of additional aspects, I treat the topic in detail in my forthcoming essay on 'Vom Herrschaftsverband zum Traditionsverband? Schriftdenkmäler in öffentlichen Begegnungen von bischöflichem Stadtherrn und Rat im spätmittelalterlichen Basel', *Frühmittelalterliche Studien,* 38 (2004), 449-491. I would like to thank my colleague and friend Christoph Dartmann for his inspiring comments and support; Christina Oppel and Ulrich Fischer for their proven, again spontaneously assured assistance in the translation of a text into English; and, most particularly, Jacqueline van Leeuwen, whose organizational energy and kindness turned the conference at Leuven into a great experience.
2. Cf. recently Gerd Althoff, *Die Macht der Rituale: Symbolik und Herrschaft im Mittelalter* (Darmstadt, 2003), and the bibliography there.
3. On encounters and similar forms of social interaction as sources for the respective organization of communities, see Erving Goffman, *Encounters: Two Studies in the Sociology of Interaction* (Indianapolis, IN, 1961; repr. London, 1972).
4. For the concept of 'hot' and 'cold' societies, see Claude Lévi-Strauss, *"Primitive" und "Zivilisierte". Nach Gesprächen aufgezeichnet von Georges Charbonnier* (Zurich, 1972), p. 34.

actors in their contemporaries' writings, related back on traditions. For my field of research, premodern Basel, the turbulent tenure of Otto of Grandson, who was bishop between 1306 and 1309, can serve as an example. Being equipped with large benefices and estates in England, young Otto grew up at the court of King Edward I.[5] Hence, he was not only a cultural stranger in the ambience of the Upper Rhine, but also a natural enemy of the German King Albert I, the Capetian's ally against the Angevin Empire.[6] According to the rules of the game of symbolic communication, a scandal was inevitably at hand when the king came to Basel and the bishop met him for the first time to receive his investiture with the regalia. In the dramatic pause after Otto had fallen on his knees to demonstrate his plea, Albert only said dryly: 'What does this schoolboy want?' – One reason why, from this stage, the scene had a different ending, was that the Habsburg only spoke German and the Savoyarde only spoke French. But the main reason was lying in their interpretors' presence of mind, the citizen of Basel Hugo zer Sunnen. The following is a translation from the chronicle of Matthias of Neuenburg:

> ... the bishop, who didn't understand him [the king, Ch.F.W.], but who believed, that he rejected him, said enraged: 'Qui di, qui di?' But, as Hugo saw the bishop's fury – who was young and hot-tempered –, he respectfully addressed the bishop in French: 'Mylord, our lord the king says that he will gladly invest you tomorrow and that he would like to do everything that he is obliged to for the Church of Basel', and the bishop answered, while bowing himself, 'Gramersi!'[7]

5. On Otto of Grandson, Bishop of Basel, see Johann Baptist Villiger, *Das Bistum Basel zur Zeit Johanns XXII., Benedikts XII. und Klemens VI. (1316 – 1352)*, Analecta Gregoriana, 15 (Rome, 1939), pp. 4-7; *Helvetia Sacra*, I/1, ed. Albert Bruckner (Bern, 1972), pp. 184-85; on the Grandson family, cf. Esther Rowland Clifford, *A Knight of Great Renown: The Life and Times of Othon de Grandson* (Chicago, IL, 1961).
6. Cf. Fritz Trautz, *Die Könige von England und das Reich, 1272–1377. Mit einem Rückblick auf ihr Verhältnis zu den Staufern* (Heidelberg, 1961), pp. 180-86.
7. My translation. Matthias of Neuenburg, *Chronica*, ed. Adolf Hofmeister, MGH SSrerGerm, n.s. 4 (Berlin, [2]1955), p. 68: 'Hic Otto, cum rex ipsum nollet de suis regalibus investire et alias esset infestus eidem, quadam vice rege existente Basilee in curia Monachorum in monte Sancti Petri assumptis servitoribus suis accessit regem ac genu flexus coram eo per Hugonem ad Solem scientem Gallicum per regem se peciit investiri. Rex enim Gallicum, episcopus vero Theutonicum nesciverunt. Venit autem episcopus eo animo, quod si eum rennuisset investire, quod eum voluit occidisse. Petente ergo Hugone in Theutonico a rege episcopum humiliter investiri, rege vero respondente vulgariter, quid vellet iste scolaris, episcopus non intelligens, sed credens eum recusasse iratus dixit: "Qui di, qui di?" Hugo vero videns furiam episcopi – erat enim iuvenis et animosus – mansuete dixit episcopo in Gallico: "Domine, dominus noster rex dixit, quod cras libenter velit vos investire et omnia facere, ad que ecclesie Basiliensi tenetur", et episcopus se inclinans dixit: "Gramersi!" Rex autem videns motum episcopi illico recessit, non ingrediens amplius Basileam, sed contra illos durius est incensus'.

Being confronted with a diplomatic catastrophy, the local hero rescued the situation for the moment being, by translating an imaginary answer that would have been the appropriate one according to the ritual tradition. His bilingualism, as well as his knowledge of the courtly speech and ritual procedure enabled the citizen of Basel to solve the crisis with the necessary flexibility.[8]

As we can see from this example, established traditions did not automatically lead to a petrification of communication, but rather worked as prerequisites for flexibility and innovations. It seems to me that this is a characteristic of symbolic communication in the late Middle Ages. It's basis consisted in the increasing growth of literacy since the twelfth century.[9] In the course of this process, the use of literacy, as well as the differentiation in many patterns of life, contributed to the development of the complex structures that formed the late medieval world. It has to be stressed that literacy hasn't brought symbolic communication to an end by means of rituals etcetera.[10] From then on, those rituals were often documented in notarial documents with notable detailedness by the notaries and town scribes present.[11] The interaction addressed between literary and performative modes in the symbolic communication of medieval political communities is the object of investigation of the research project A1 in the collaborative research centre 496 at Münster. Research results in this field have shown that the value and the text message of documents often become more intelligible, if the document is also interpreted

8. Cf. Thomas Behrmann, 'Zum Wandel der öffentlichen Anrede im Spätmittelalter', in *Formen und Funktionen öffentlicher Kommunikation im Mittelalter*, ed. Gerd Althoff, Vorträge und Forschungen, 51 (Stuttgart, 2001), pp. 291-317; Gabriele Müller-Oberhäuser, '*With cortays speche*: Verbale Höflichkeit in den mittelenglischen Courtesy Books', in *Pragmatische Dimensionen mittelalterlicher Schriftkultur*, eds. Christel Meier, Volker Honemann, Hagen Keller, and Rudolf Suntrup, Münstersche Mittelalter-Schriften, 79 (Munich, 2002), pp. 211-31.

9. Michael T. Clanchy, *From Memory to Written Record: England 1066–1307*, 2nd ed. (Oxford, 1993); Hagen Keller, 'Die Entwicklung der europäischen Schriftkultur im Spiegel der mittelalterlichen Überlieferung. Beobachtungen und Überlegungen', in *Geschichte und Geschichtsbewußtsein. Festschrift Karl-Ernst Jeismann zum 65. Geburtstag*, eds. Paul Leidinger and Dieter Metzler (Münster, 1990), pp. 171-204; id., 'Vom 'heiligen Buch' zur 'Buchführung': Lebensfunktionen der Schrift im Mittelalter', *Frühmittelalterliche Studien*, 26 (1992), 1-31; cf. the contributions on the Latin Christendom in *Pragmatic Literacy, East and West: 1200–1330*, ed. Richard Britnell (Woodbridge, Suffolk, 1997).

10. Hagen Keller, 'Schriftgebrauch und Symbolhandeln in der öffentlichen Kommunikation: Aspekte des gesellschaftlich-kulturellen Wandels vom 5. bis zum 13. Jahrhundert', *Frühmittelalterliche Studien*, 37 (2003), 1-24.

11. Cf., for example, Christoph Friedrich Weber, '*Ces grands privilèges*: The Symbolic Use of Written Documents in the Foundation and Institutionalization Processes of Medieval Universities', *History of Universities*, 19/1 (2004), 12-62.

as an object of performative processes in its special context of symbolic communication.[12]

I would like to follow this main idea for an investigation of public encounters between the city council and the episcopal lord in late medieval Basel.[13] Previous scholarly work has stated that encounters like the annual approbation of the city council or the great processions that were carried out until the Reformation ended up in empty formalism. At the latest from the middle of the fourteenth century, when the city was powerful enough to act independently, the public services for the bishop became more and more routine jobs.[14]

Contrary to this view, I would like to argue that the symbolic communication between the bishop and the city council had rather experienced transitions and kept a lot of its significance. One main reason for this was the fact that the legitimation of the city council was combined with the granting of a charter.

In 1218, King Frederick II confirmed in his golden bull for Bishop Henry of Thun, 'that the people of Basel shall hitherto establish no

12. For recent examples of work from the research project, see above ns 1, 10, 11, and Hagen Keller, 'Otto der Große urkundet im Bodenseegebiet. Inszenierungen der „Gegenwart des Herrschers" in einer vom König selten besuchten Landschaft', in *Mediaevalia Augiensia: Forschungen zur Geschichte des Mittelalters*, ed. Jürgen Petersohn, Vorträge und Forschungen, 54 (Stuttgart, 2001), pp. 205-45; Peter Worm, 'Beobachtungen zum Privilegierungsakt am Beispiel einer Urkunde Pippins II. von Aquitanien', *Archiv für Diplomatik*, 49 (2003), 15-48; Hagen Keller and Christoph Dartmann, 'Inszenierungen von Ordnung und Konsens: Privileg und Statutenbuch in der symbolischen Kommunikation mittelalterlicher Rechtsgemeinschaften', in *Zeichen – Rituale – Werte*. Internationales Kolloquium des Sonderforschungsbereichs 496 an der Westfälischen Wilhelms-Universität Münster, ed. Gerd Althoff, Symbolische Kommunikation und gesellschaftliche Wertesysteme, 3 (Münster, 2004), pp. 201-223; Christoph Dartmann, 'Schrift im Ritual. Der Amtseid des Podestà auf den geschlossenen Statutencodex der italienischen Stadtkommune', *Zeitschrift für Historische Forschung*, 31 (2004), 169-204; Christoph Friedrich Weber, 'Schriftstücke in der symbolischen Kommunikation zwischen Bischof Johann von Venningen (1458–1478) und der Stadt Basel', *Frühmittelalterliche Studien*, 37 (2003), 357-84; id., 'Suitable for Crown and Gown: The Ritual Context of the Royal Privileges for the University of Paris', in *Strategies of Writing. Texts and Trust in Medieval Europe. Papers from the Fifth Utrecht Symposium on Medieval Litaracy, organized by the Pioneer Project Verschriftelijking in collaboration with the Historiches Seminar der Universität zu Köln, Utrecht 28-29 November 2002*, eds. Marco Mostert, Petra Schulte and Irene van Reuswoude, Utrecht Studies in Medieval Literacy, 12 (Turnhout, in print). See also the proceedings, gathered in *Frühmittelalterliche Studien*, 38 (2004), of the conference held at Münster in June 2003 under the title 'Öffentlichkeit und Schriftdenkmal in der mittelalterlichen Gesellschaft'.
13. The general history of late medieval Basel by Rudolf Wackernagel, *Geschichte der Stadt Basel*, 3 vols (Basel, 1907–1924), remains indispensable. See also Hans Rudolf Guggisberg, *Basel in the Sixteenth Century: Aspects of the City Republic before, during, and after the Reformation* (St. Louis, MO, 1982).
14. René Teuteberg, *Basler Geschichte*, 2nd ed. (Basel, 1988), p. 115.

council or any other new institution, independent from the name by which it will be known, without the consent and the will of the bishop'.[15] Based on this principle, Bishop Henry's successors forced the integration of city council and guilds into the government of the town of Basel to their terms. On behalf of bishop and chapter, the bishop's *ministeriales* already held offices in the governance of town and bishopric. One can see from later sources that symbolic communication in this political community of bishop, chapter, and nobility consisted mainly of rituals and gestures which had to express the bishop's role as temporal and spiritual lord. The matrix of this symbolic communication was the *ecclesia Basiliensis*, the buildings, the liturgy, the saints, and the values of the church of Basel.[16]

To take an example, a vassal of the bishopric had a ritual encounter with his episcopal lord when he became a knight. Before his dubbing to knighthood, he could ask his lord for a customary gift of five pounds of the currency of Basel. When he had been dubbed, the new knight had to enter the cathedral and lay his sword on the altar of the Virgin Mary. This altar stood at the jube, at the border between the choir and the laymen's part of the church. In turn, the bishop had to buy a new sword and consecrate it, wearing his pontifical vestments, over the altar of the Virgin in the provost's chapel. During this ceremony, the knight should kneel before the altar and finally receive his new sword out of the bishop's hands.[17]

---

15. My translation. *Urkundenbuch der Stadt Basel*, eds. Rudolf Wackernagel, Rudolf Thommen, August Huber, and Johannes Haller, 11 vols (Basel, 1890–1910), 1, no. 92, p. 62: 'Ad maiorem autem gratie ac dilectionis nostre circa memoratum episcopum evidentiam nolumus, immo sub plena gratie nostre interminatione omnino inhibemus, ne Basilienses de cetero consilium vel aliquam institutionem novam quocumque nomine possit appellari faciant aut instituant sine episcopi sui assensu et voluntate'.

16. Cf. *Der Basler Münsterschatz*, ed. Historisches Museum Basel (Basel, 2001).

17. *Monuments de l'histoire de l'ancien évêché de Bâle*, ed. Joseph Trouillat, 5 vols (vol 5 ed. Louis Vautrey) (Porrentruy, 1852–1867), 4, no. 3, p. 10: 'Ein man oder dienstman, wenn er Ritter werden wil, der sol vorderen an den Byschof stùr, und ist Im der Byschoff schuldig fünf pfunt Baszler ze geben. Wird er erlich Ritter und kumpt wider, so soll er sin ritter schwert uf Unser lieben Fröwen Altar ze Basel opferen, das sol da beliben, und sol Im der Bischof ein nùws ritter schwert koufen biss an drii pfunt und ym das von Unser Lieben frovwen Altar im Tůmstifft in sinem bischöfflichen Gewand ansegenen, das ouch der Ritter uff sinen Kniwen demüttiglich empfahen sol zů einem zeichen, dass umb Gottes Ere den Cristen glouben helfe retten und die priesterschaft, Wittiwen und weisen helffe schirmen'. Cf. *Das Bischofs und Dienstmannenrecht von Basel in deutscher Aufzeichnung des XIII Jahrhunderts*, ed. Wilhelm Wackernagel (Basel, 1852). On the two altars of Our Lady, see *Das Hochstift Basel im ausgehenden Mittelalter (Quellen und Forschungen)*, ed. Konrad W. Hieronimus (Basel, 1938), pp. 406-9 and 420-22.

Since the twelfth century, the liturgical frame and the blessing of the sword were common features in the ritual action of knighting.[18] More important for our questions is the fact that the ritual decribed created loyality between the bishop and the group of men who had both feudal and political duties in regard to him. Notably, the encounters took place in front of the altars of the Virgin Mary who was the patroness of cathedral and bishopric and therefore figuratively the female overlord of the whole community. The bishop's authority as a temporal lord was not contradictory to his status as cleric, but was rather supported by his liturgical appearance.[19]

The complex of cathedral, bishop's palace, cathedral square, and other surrounding buildings, all located on the steeply hill, called *auf Burg*, above the Rhine, was the centre of ritual performances for the episcopal *curia*.[20] On all Candlemas-days, especially on *Purificatio Mariae*, the noble officials of the bishopric had to deliver lights for 'Unser frowen kilchen' ('the church of Our Lady').[21] During the special liturgy of the feast, the candles were consecrated and carried through the cathedral and over the cathedral-square in solemn procession.[22]

In the course of the thirteenth century, the corporated citizens of Basel, like the guilds which were appointed by the bishops, were integrated into

18. See Elsbet Orth, 'Formen und Funktionen der höfischen Rittererhebung', in *Curialitas: Studien zu Grundfragen der höfisch-ritterlichen Kultur*, ed. Josef Fleckenstein, Veröffentlichungen des Max-Planck-Instituts für Geschichte, 100 (Göttingen, 1990), pp. 128-70, esp. 141-53.

19. Cf., in this sense, the appearance of the bishop in the initial miniature of the *Lehenbuch* of the bishopric of Basel from 1441; Hans Rott, *Quellen und Forschungen zur südwestdeutschen und schweizerischen Kunstgeschichte im XV. und XVI. Jahrhundert: 3. Der Oberrhein, Text* (Stuttgart, 1938), pp. 130-33; *Der Basler Münsterschatz*, fig. 195. On household and administration of the bishops of Basel in the later Middle Ages see Kurt Weissen, 'Die weltliche Verwaltung des Fürstbistums Basel am Ende des Spätmittelalters und der Ausbau der Landesherrschaft', in *La donation de 999 et l'histoire médiévale de l'ancien Évêché de Bâle*, ed. Jean-Claude Rebetez (Porrentruy, 2002), pp. 213-40.

20. *Das Hochstift Basel*, ed. Hieronimus; Christian Wurstisen, *Beschreibung des Basler Münsters und seiner Umgebung*, ed. Rudolf Wackernagel, *Beiträge zur vaterländischen Geschichte, ed. Historische und Antiquarische Gesellschaft zu Basel*, 12 (1888), 399-522; cf. Mathias Kälble, 'Basel', in *Höfe und Residenzen im spätmittelalterlichen Reich: Ein dynastisch-topographisches Handbuch, 2: Residenzen*, eds. Werner Paravicini, Jan Hirschbiegel, and Jörg Wettlaufer, Residenzenforschung, 15.I (Ostfildern, 2003), pp. 39-41.

21. *Monuments de l'histoire de l'ancien évêché de Bâle*, 4, no. 3, p. 16: 'Und zů allen Liechtmess tagen, ist man gebunden Kerzen ze geben, in Unser frowen kilchen, den manen und oberen Amptlùten als einen Prelaten, den dienstmannen und Mittelamptlùten als einem Caplan. Welhelm man oder dienstman obern und mitlen Amptlùten das verzigen würd, der mag ein Kerzen in sǒlicher schwere ab dem fron Altar nehmen, und sy ungestraft dannen tragen. Aber den belehneten und nidren Amptlùten gezimpt soliche friheit nit; wer aber personlich nit zegegen ist, dem ist man das nit schuldig'.

22. *Das Hochstift Basel*, ed. Hieronimus, pp. 138-40.

this nexus of symbolic communication. They also had to give money, wax, and oil for the illumination of the cathedral. The so-called 'Bezünden des Münsters' referred to the value system behind the acitivities of the political community. The four oldest guild charters, given between 1226 and 1260, state explicitly that this duty has to be carried out for the honour of God, the Virgin, and the saints.[23]

In the middle of the thirteenth century, the ritual frame for public encounters between the episcopal lord and the city council was established as well. Its endurance until the close of the Middle Ages was founded in the interaction between the confirmation of a privilege and a public ritual. Since the 1260s, every new bishop of Basel confirmed the so-called *Basler Handfeste* on the occasion of his first encounter with the council.[24] The document was sealed by him, the chapter, and the council. In order to realize the royal provisions of 1218 mentioned above, implying the bishop's right of appointing the city council, the *Handfeste* sets out the proceedings for two kinds of encounters of bishop and council. The first encounter was directed at guaranteeing a promissory oath taken by both sides in order to ensure each other's rights and the bishop's lifelong promise to provide the town with a regiment. The procedure of the election of the city council was set by the *Handfeste*. According to it, the election preceded the two parties' second encounter, the annual public appointment of the council on the Sunday before Midsummer Day.[25]

On the preceding Saturday, three candidates for the mayor's office had been elected. After this, representatives of the old council moved to the bishop's court to present them. The lord bishop was supplicated to accept the persons elected and to invest one of them into his office on the following day. In order to stress the plead, town sergeants brought four cans of wine to the bishop. On Sunday morning, the old council was assembled by means of bells and went over to the bishop's court in order to have a joint breakfast. Afterwards, the council would meet the bishop who was accompanied by the chapter and his ministerial officials in front of the cathedral. Then the election of the electoral college for the new councillors, the so called *Kieser*, took place in the house of the cathedral's fabric. Now, the scenery became public. Those involved went outside to the square in front of the cathedral where they were awaited by the peo-

23. *Urkundenbuch der Stadt Basel* 1, no. 108, p. 77; no. 199, p. 143; no. 221, p. 159; no. 388, p. 291. Cf. Traugott Geering, *Handel und Industrie der Stadt Basel. Zunftwesen und Wirtschaftsgeschichte bis zum Ende des XVII. Jahrhunderts* (Basel, 1886), pp. 16, 23, and 98-99.
24. *Urkundenbuch der Stadt Basel*, 4, no. 134, pp. 125-26.
25. For what follows see Weber, 'Vom Herrschaftsverband zum Traditionsverband?'

ple. The town scribe read out loud the *Handfeste* and further privileges
to the citizens and to the representatives of the University of Basel who
all had been summoned by ringing bells and town criers. The bishop took
seat on a throne and the names of the electors were read out. Those present swore on the plenarium of the cathedral's treasure to do their duty.
After the election inside the house mentioned, they returned and the former mayor now asked the bishop – with reference to the *Handfeste* – to
give a new regiment to the city. The names of the newly elected councillors were read out and they also came forward to the bishop and swore
their oath of office on the *Kaiser-Heinrichs-Kreuz*, a cross given to the
cathedral by Emperor Henry II, which contained particles of the cross
and blood of Jesus Christ. On another day, the citizens also swore an oath
to the new regiment.

Of course, some elements of the elaborate ritual, only sketched here in
outline, have changed in the course of time. On the whole, it gives a typical example for the process of constituting a city's regiment in late
medieval times. One of its main structural elements, the change from
closed rooms in which the 'ruling class' came to its decisions to the public place where the decision was made public has also been observed by
Jacqueline van Leeuwen for the *wetsvernieuwing* of Flemish towns.[26]
Another comparative aspect is the commonly used practice of gifts of
wine, in the town on the Upper Rhine as well as in the Low Countries.[27]

Although the *Handfeste* did not even set out these forms of its ritual
enactment in writing, the charter's constant presence and the linking of
both document and ritual were an ideal solution to constitute a political
order permanently. But the later history of Basel also shows the weak
point of this system that was done according to the possibilities offered
by medieval *Staatlichkeit* in general and the rulership of lord-bishops in
particular. In times of conflict, the system was endangered by being bound
to the bishop's intentions.

Between 1365 and 1367, such a conflict was carried out between the
town on one side and the bishop and the chapter on the other side. Its ini-

26. Jacoba van Leeuwen, 'De wisseling van de macht. Een onderzoek naar de betekenis van de wetsvernieuwing in Gent, Brugge en Ieper (1379–1493)' (Ph.D. thesis,
Katholieke Universiteit Leuven, 2002), p. 543.

27. The common use and the meanings of such practices have been revealed by
Valentin Groebner's studies. Cf., most recently, Valentin Groebner, 'The City Guard's
Salute: Legal and Illegal, Public and Private Gifts in the Swiss Confederation around
1500', in *Negotiating the Gift: Pre-Modern Figurations of Exchange*, eds. Gadi Algazi,
Valentin Groebner, and Bernhard Jussen, Veröffentlichungen des Max-Planck-Instituts für
Geschichte, 188 (Göttingen, 2003), pp. 247-67, and the contribution by Mario Damen
in this volume.

tiation resulted in the council's behaviour in the interim after Bishop
Johann Senn von Münsingen's death, which took place on 30 June in
1365.[28] As his *Handfeste* was now invalidated and as the chapter made
several concessions to the council, the latter acted in doing something
that actually ran counter to its sworn duty of mutually guaranteeing
rights[29]: mayor and council issued statutes that intervened with the rights
of the clergy. Above all, their tax exemption was touched. Of course, the
chapter protested against this intervention. The protest was mainly
directed towards the public character of the council's proceedings, for
the new statutes had been announced publicly and solemnly in front of
the town hall 'per cridam et proclamacionem'.[30] When the chapter threatened on 7 April 1366 to issue an interdict by means of a publicly read
notarial instrument, the town reacted by means of a symbolic gesture.[31]
Its provocative character only becomes intelligible when seen within the
ritual framework of the *Handfeste*. The members of the city council and
the members of the guilds entered the cathedral and broke off all the
lights and candles.[32] Though the citizens had to provide the church with
lights and candles, the deed did not only express their protest, but also
signalled an insulting revocation of their symbolically expressed duty to
the church of Basel with regard to the threatening anathema. By means
of this, the dispute which had in the beginning only dealt with rights to
power and public enactment, now reached a level on which the conflicting parties referred to the system of the values of the church of Basel by
means of their actions. As the conflict and especially the town's behaviour endangered the legitimacy of those in power, the following action of
the new bishop becomes more understandable.

On 13 August 1365, pope Urban V appointed John of Vienne, whose
family belonged to the high nobility of Burgundy, as bishop of Basel.[33]
He quickly came to terms with the chapter on proceedings with the city.[34]
In April 1366, a confrontation with the council, which still consisted of
those members who had been elected when his predecessor was bishop,
came about.

---

28. *Monuments de l'histoire de l'ancien évêché de Bâle,* 4, no. 100, p. 226.
29. *Urkundenbuch der Stadt Basel,* 4, no. 299, p. 273.
30. Ibid., no. 301, p. 275.
31. Ibid., pp. 274-76.
32. *Monuments de l'histoire de l'ancien évêché de Bâle,* 4, no. 103, p. 230.
33. *Helvetia Sacra,* I/1, ed. Albert Bruckner (Bern, 1972), pp. 188-89.
34. *Monuments de l'histoire de l'ancien évêché de Bâle,* 4, p. 699; ibid., no. 103,
p. 229-33; Urkundenbuch der Stadt Basel, 4, no. 302, pp. 276-77.

The council asked for the *Handfeste* so that before the feast of St John a new council could be elected. Apparently, the councillors resorted to tradition as their justification, for not only did Bishop John denied the stipulation, but he also began the charter which he had drawn up on the matter with a summary of the issue:

> As the mayor, councillors and the community of Basel demand a certain charter on the annual public appointment of a mayor and councillors, in each year, which had been given to them by certain bishops of Basel, our predecessors, for a limited period of time, and limited to the life span of these bishops, as they say, given and sealed by their grace, now to be voluntarily granted to them as a matter of liability and to be sealed by us, although we have little inclination to do so.[35]

While he had confirmed the privileges of the towns of his principality immediately after his accession, Bishop John of Vienne in the conflict with his cathedral city made use of the *a priori* necessity of his assent to the *Handfeste* and the political system that was based on it.[36] He withheld the charter to the council, as it was – according to his own interpretation – an individual testimony of episcopal grace. Also he viewed the council as bound to him by its oath, on which grounds he viewed the decree of statutes as a breach of the privilege of 1218 and of the *Handfeste*, to which the oath was linked.[37] However, he had, at first, but little success. In June 1366, the citizens of Basel elected a new council, and performed the oath-taking rituals by themselves. The bishop, unable to ignore this, now took up new measures to bring his privilege to bear: with his privileges he turned to the emperor. On 14 September, 1366, Charles IV confirmed in a golden bull the 1218 privilege by Frederick II, adding to his confirmation that the council and the community of Basel were compelled under pain to heed the privilege.[38]

It was only after several attempts that an agreement was reached in the following year. On 23 January 1367, Bishop John handed the *Handfeste* over to the city authorities, and two months later, he absolved the town

35. My translation. *Monuments de l'histoire de l'ancien évêché de Bâle*, 4, no. 103, p. 229: 'Nam magister ciuium et consules et commune ciuitatis Basiliensis quandam litteram super deputandis annuatim magistero et consulibus, annis singulis, eis per quondam episcopos Basilienses predecessores nostros temporaliter, et ad ipsorum episcoporum vitam duntaxat, vt dicunt, concessam et de gratia sigillatam, nunc sibi quasi ex debito indebite exigunt concedendam, et etiam per nos sigillandam, licet ad hoc minime teneamur'.

36. *Monuments de l'histoire de l'ancien évêché de Bâle*, 4, no. 101-2, pp. 227-29; ibid., p. 697-98; *Urkundenbuch der Stadt Basel*, 4, no. 300, pp. 273-74.

37. Cf. *Monuments de l'histoire de l'ancien évêché de Bâle*, 4, no. 103, p. 230.

38. *Urkundenbuch der Stadt Basel*, 4, no. 305-306, pp. 278-81.

from the interdict.[39] The cathedral chapter made a special agreement with the town authorities. It was only on the 21 February 1367 that it agreed to co-seal the *Handfeste*, under the condition that the mayor, the supreme master of the guilds and council follow the document not only according to its wording, but also according to tradition.[40]

This conflict, only presented here in outline, allows insight into the interconnections posited at the beginning. Although the council, a century after the establishment of a model of symbolic communication with the lord of the city, felt powerful enough to establish law by itself and even to renew its bodies on its own account, it, nevertheless, did not want to do without the traditional form of legitimation of its power. Thus, the conflict ended with the handing over of a charter which allowed for further encounters of bishop and council within the traditional framework. This interpretation is not only a re-wording of the well-known thesis on the retention of a ritual out of routine, and its furnishing with a new, 'trendy' terminology, for the adherence to the *Handfeste* and the formal appointment of the new council was motivated by more than just medieval formalism. The example of the candles, in particular, illustrates the fact that the meaning of individual ritual elements was clearly present: a newly-developed gesture of conflict, in this case the forceful removal of the lights in the cathedral depended on a knowledge of the political implications of the illumination of the cathedral. In my view, however, the central aspect is the different reception of these rituals on the two sides. The council saw the complex of oath-taking, *Handfeste* and appointment of the council mainly as the traditional form of its confirmation. Since the final years of the fourteenth century, it had accepted the bishop's role as lord of the city in its performative form, that is, limited to the public rituals. If, however, the bishop demanded the realization of the obligations derived from oath, charter, and ritual in a different context, conflict was imminent. At the bottom of this transition in the reception or interpretation of symbolic communication and its binding character was the increasing power of the city which came to outstrip that of the bishop.

Throughout the fifteenth century, both sides kept up the handing over of the *Handfeste* and the appointment of the council. At first glance, it seems almost paradoxical that the bishop or the council were hardly ever present any more at these traditional incidents of their encounter. And

39. Ibid., no. 309, pp. 287-88; ibid., no. 312-13, pp. 291-92; ibid., no. 315, pp. 294-95.

40. Ibid., no. 314, pp. 292-94.

yet, this is a natural consequence of the development that had already been heralded. The bishops, who had by now taken up their residence in the small towns of Delsberg and Pruntrut, had a representative take up their role.[41] And when Bishop John of Venningen, in 1466, presented to the council a catalogue of grievances, he also included the fact that the councillors tried to elude themselves from their oath to the bishop by means of staying away from the ceremony.[42] Instead, new forms of public encounters between the bishop and the council appeared. Thus, the parties met before arbitral courts, where they acted out their conflicts and where, naturally, their roles were not as neatly fixed as at their traditional encounters.

Consequently, the city council still faced – in the fifteenth century – the problem of acting out political power against the bishop and the cathedral chapter, without wanting to renounce the charter in the ritual. Joining the Swiss Confederation offered a solution for the city, for, in this political system the connection between the individual communities was also based on a ritual in the course of which a charter, the so called *Bundesbrief* ('letter of confederation') was sworn in public.[43] The letter of confederation, which was sealed by the envoys of Basel and the confederate communities on 9 July 1501 at Lucerne, was to be read out in front of, and subsequently sworn by, the council, citizens, and envoys of the other confederate communities every five years.[44] This 'eternal covenant' began to replace the *Handfeste* at Basel, which was handed out to the city for the last time by Bishop Christoph of Utenheim (1502-1527) on 8 May 1506.[45]

The ritual performance of the oath of confederation can only be understood with respect to that of the *Handfeste*. On the one hand, it took over unperilous, legitimizing elements from local tradition, such as the cult of

41. Cf. Katharina Simon-Muscheid, 'Delsberg', in *Höfe und Residenzen im spätmittelalterlichen Reich*, pp. 125-26; ead., 'Pruntrut', in ibid., pp. 465-69. The representative usually came from the ranks of the chapter; *Basler Chroniken, 5*, ed. August Bernoulli (Leipzig, 1895), p. 83; *Monuments de l'histoire de l'ancien évêché de Bâle, 3*, no. 288, p. 470; *Das Hochstift Basel*, ed. Hieronimus, p. 291.

42. Josef Stöcklin, *Johann VI. von Venningen: Bischof von Basel 17. Mai 1458 bis 20. Dezember 1478* (Solothurn, 1902), pp. 61-82.

43. William E. Rappard, *Du renouvellement des pactes confédéraux (1351–1798) (Beschwörung und Erneuerung der Bünde)*, Zeitschrift für Schweizerische Geschichte: Beiheft 2 (Zurich, 1944); cf. Roger Sablonier, 'The Swiss Confederation', in *The New Cambridge Medieval History, 7*, ed. Christopher Allmand (Cambridge, 1998), pp. 645-70.

44. *Urkundenbuch der Stadt Basel, 9*, no. 272, pp. 196-206. Cf. Michael Jucker, *Gesandte, Schreiber, Akten. Politische Kommunikation auf eidgenössischen Tagsatzungen im Spätmittelalter* (Zurich, 2004).

45. *Urkundenbuch der Stadt Basel, 9*, no. 330, pp. 287-89.

the diocesan saint Emperor Henry II, on whose feast day, in 1501, the city authorities of Basel had the letter of confederation read out publicly and sworn to for the first time.[46] On the other hand it was a conscious renunciation from those ritual forms which had had a particularly close association to episcopal rule. Thus, the cathedral and the cathedral square, the traditional place for the ritual performance of rule over the city, were averted now. Instead, since 1501, the public reading and swearing of the letter of confederation took place at the corn market in front of the new town hall. There, the hall of the city council was inaugurated on 12 March, 1521, with a session at which the council declared that it was no longer bound to the *Handfeste* and did not want to swear to the bishop any more and to conduct reelections autonomously from now on.[47] Since 1521, a new public dramatisation of the political community of Basel by means of an autonomous election of the city council and the oath of confederation was established, in which the confederation had in a way taken up the position of the bishop. While, before, the citizens had seen how their lord, the bishop, had confirmed the city authorities, they were now faced with a new type of authority, the representatives of which occupied the same rank as the confederate envoys which stood together with them on the same stands.

Westfälische Wilhelms-Universität Münster

---

46. See the classic account by Albert Bruckner, 'Basels Weg zum Schweizerbund', in id. – Edgar Bonjour, *Basel und die Eidgenossen: Geschichte ihrer Beziehungen zur Erinnerung an Basels Eintritt in den Schweizerbund, 1501* (Basel, 1951), pp. 9-143, at 128-32. On the reinterpretation of local traditions as the cult of the Emperor Saint, see most recently Stefan Hess, 'Zwischen Verehrung und Versenkung: Zum Nachleben Kaiser Heinrichs II. in Basel', *Basler Zeitschrift für Geschichte und Altertumskunde,* 102 (2002), 83-143.

47. Wackernagel, *Geschichte der Stadt Basel,* 3 (Basel, 1924), pp. 301-3.

Katell LAVÉANT

LE ROI ET SON DOUBLE:
A ROYAL ENTRY TO LATE-MEDIEVAL ABBEVILLE[1]

Although numerous mentions of royal entries in the 15th and 16th centuries in northern France have been preserved, as well as many descriptions of these events, very few texts of the plays performed during these entries remain. This is a problem when we want to study symbolic communication in this context, since we can usually rely only on the descriptions of the settings, of the subject of the plays, and of the reaction of the spectators if recorded, but not on the content of the texts. In many cases, we have therefore only external elements to understand what symbolic communication was about and how it worked in a royal entry. Moreover, the descriptions are reported in most cases by a chronicler of the sovereign or a citizen of the welcoming city, and these observers are by definition never neutral. The bias of the observer prevents a full view of the event in all its aspects.

The transcription made by Alcius Ledieu at the beginning of the 20th century of a short play from 1531 is therefore very precious in order to know what kind of play could be performed during a royal entry. This text is a short dialogue, called *La Declaracion des misteres faictz à l'entrée de la tres noble et excellente dame et Royne de France madame Alyenor.*[2] It was performed to welcome in Abbeville on the 19th of December 1531 Eleanor of Habsburg, who was newly wed to Francis I. The whole account of the ceremony, including the text of the *Declaracion*, was kept in the city's register of deliberations and the accounting books for the year 1531. The copy Ledieu made from these documents is our only witness of what was the text, since the original manuscripts were destroyed during World War II.

---

1. I would like to express my gratitude to Jelle Koopmans, whose valuable advices on the form as well as on the content of this article were of a great help. I also want to thank Estelle Doudet for the useful informations about George Chastelain she kindly gave me, as well as Suzanne Aalberse for her linguistic advices. I translated some french excerpts in english: those coming from archives, chronicles or poems of the 15th and 16th centuries. I did not translate the quotation from modern scholars nor the play edited at the end of this article.

2. Alcius Ledieu, ed., 'Entrée de la reine Éléonore d'Autriche à Abbeville le 19 décembre 1531', *Mélanges d'histoire locale, lectures faites à la société d'émulation d'Abbeville de 1895 à 1900* (Paris, 1901), pp. 367-413. From now on, I will call it the *Declaracion*.

This *Declaracion* is therefore of a great importance in regard with the history of theatre in northern France, given the shortage of original playing texts, and it is worth looking at the reasons why this particular one was kept. Moreover, this text allows us to take another angle to study symbolic communication in royal entries in general, and particularly in this royal entry of Eleanor, for it sets up a complex strategy of communication on and from the stage toward the different categories of audience. I will therefore reproduce Ledieu's edition (this edition being difficult to find), since it does not seem to present any incoherence, from what we can judge (see appendix). I will analyze its content as well as the historical context in which it was played, to see what communication is and how it works in this particular instance. In order to judge of the peculiarity of this specific text, I will also compare it with other plays of the time dealing with the same striking point, that is to say, the way the king is staged and addressed in the play. This will allow us to understand better the aims of this play in regard to the relationship built during this entry between the queen, the king and the city of Abbeville, through symbolic communication.

Eleanor had just got married to Francis I when she came to Abbeville, since the wedding took place on the 7th of July 1530. Thanks to Ledieu's article, we have in hand some excerpts from the aldermen's register of deliberation and the accounts for the year 1531. The queen enters the city on the 19th of December 1531 without the king, who is to arrive the next day, but with the sons and daughters of Francis I, several important people of the kingdom, and her suite. Since she has never entered the city before, the ceremony is supposed to be especially in her honour, whereas the king, who has already entered the city officially in 1517, will be welcomed in a simpler way. For instance, he will not receive any present, which is also the case for his daughters, but Eleanor receives a precious candy-box. The register of deliberation states, on the 11th of December 1531, that:

> 'Deliberé a esté qu'il ne sera faict aulcun present au Roy, consideré qu'il n'y a que la royne quy fache entrée, ny aussy pareillement aux deux filles dudict seigneur.[3]

Thus, since the traditions of the royal entry do not allow the city to prepare a special ceremony for the king, the entry of the queen becomes the major event of this royal visit and the city concentrates on this ceremony to display the most sumptuous pageantry. On this day, Eleanor enters the

---

3. *'It has been decided that the king will not receive any present, since it is only the queen who enters [officially] the city, nor will the daughters of the aforesaid lord'*: Registre aux délibérations de l'Échevinage, ed. A. Ledieu, *op. cit.*, p. 382.

city under a canopy carried by several aldermen, with the sound of canons brought at the entrance of the city for the occasion. At the gate stands a stage where the *Declaracion* is played for her. Then she goes through the city where five other stages are placed, and where she can attend short plays on her way to her accommodation.

Our *Declaracion* is an allegorical dialogue of 262 lines, in which the city claims her allegiance to the king and therefore the queen, as well as a presentation and an explanation of the five short plays Eleanor is going to attend. Two characters: the 'Seigneur Souverain' and the 'Dame Souveraine', appear on stage, debating on the difference between a good and a bad marriage inspired by the story of Pyramus and Thisbe (obviously refering to the recent wedding of Eleanor). They arrive then in front of the third character, a gentle young girl named Abbeville, and ask her to explain the meaning of the tableaux that are displayed further. Abbeville greets the royal couple and explains what are these tableaux. These are, we can assume from the text and the registers, some tableaux vivants, that is to say silent illustrations with real actors. Indeed, the city feels the need to provide to the queen a play that will explain the meaning of the tableaux, which would not be necessary if the characters on the different stages were able to deliver a speech about the symbolic meaning of the scene they are placed in. Moreover, the excerpts of the accounts edited by Ledieu speak of 'cinq escharfaulx sur lesquelz ont esté *demonstrez* aucuns hystoires et joyeulx misteres' and of the 'mistere prins sur ledict psealme de "Dominus regit" pour *monstrer* par personnages sur les cinq escharfaulx mencionnez cy devant'.[4] These terms: 'monstrer' and 'demonstrer', are usually those used in the manuscripts to describe a play performed without speaking, only with gestures ('par signes'); this is confirmed for instance in the description of a 'mystère mimé' for the entry of Charles VII to Paris in 1437: 'Item devant la Trinité estoit la Passion [...]. Et ne parloient riens ceux qui ce faisoient, mais le monstroient par jeu de mistere'.[5]

The aim of the *Declaracion* that is performed at the gates of the city is thus to reveal the meaning of the following scaffolds placed in several streets of the city. Each of the five tableaux illustrates a part of Psalm 22,

4. *"five scaffolds on which have been demonstrated some stories and joyful mystery plays"* and *"a mystery play inspired from the aforesaid psalm 'Dominus regit' in order to show [the play] with characters on the five aforesaid scaffolds"*: A. Ledieu, *op. cit.*, p. 394 and 405 (the italics are mine).

5. *'Before the [Hospital of the] Trinity there was the Passion [...]. And nothing was spoken by those who portrayed this, but all was shown through playacting'*. Cited and translated by Donald Perret, 'The Meaning of the Mystery: From *Tableaux* to Theatre in the French Royal Entry', *Moving subjects. Processional Performance in the Middle Ages and the Renaissance* (Amsterdam, 2001), p. 203.

which gives its structure to the *Declaracion*.[6] The first tableau depicts Abbeville and the region of the Somme as a *locus amoenus* under the rule of the king, since the *Dominus* who *regit me* (line 110) is in fact the king, 'le tres crestien Roy François' [*the very christian king François*] (l. 113); the second tableau evokes war and how the king guided the city (*deduxit me* l. 142) to a peaceful state; the third tableau repeats the faith of the city in the king's guidance, symbolized by the *virga tuas, et baculus* (l. 176); the fourth tableau deals with the sacraments given through coronation and marriage (*impiguasti* l. 215); the fifth tableau (the only one not quoting directly the Latin text) discusses grace and mercy ('Je doibz faire misericorde' [*I have to show mercy*] l. 246). In these five tableaux where the king is put on a par with the subject of the Psalm, God himself, four major points are expressed. Firstly Abbeville reasserts her loyalty to the king (first and third scaffolds), secondly the city praises his good caretaking of the kingdom (second scaffold), thirdly Abbeville claims the legitimacy of the king, anointed in Reims by the saint phial and thereby the legitimacy of the new queen through marriage (fourth scaffold), and finally the city asks the queen – who is invested with the power of the king – to be merciful and to free the prisoners of the jail of Abbeville (fifth scaffold).

The use of Biblical references and of an exegesis of the Psalm according to the political context of the royal entry is one of the basic elements for the plays performed in such an event[7] and is therefore not the most striking element of this text. More interesting is the way the play presents itself as a mirror of the real entry and the system of symbolic communication it thus establishes with the different types of spectators.

The scheme of communication is quite complex. One complicating factor is the fact that one character can suggest several referents. The character of Abbeville in particular suggests three different groups of ref-

---

6. *Biblia sacra iuxta Vulgatam versionem*, Ps XXII:

22:1 Psalmus David/Dominus regit me et nihil mihi deerit

22:2 in loco pascuae ibi me conlocavit/super aquam refectionis educavit me

22:3 animam meam convertit/deduxit me super semitas iustitiae propter nomen suum

22:4 nam et si ambulavero in medio umbrae mortis non timebo mala quoniam tu mecum es/virga tua et baculus tuus ipsa me consolata sunt

22:5 parasti in conspectu meo mensam adversus eos qui tribulant me/inpinguasti in oleo caput meum et calix meus inebrians quam praeclarus est

22:6 et misericordia tua subsequitur me omnibus diebus vitae meae et ut inhabitem in domo Domini in longitudinem dierum.

7. See the typology of the themes exploited in the entries established by Christian de Mérindol, 'Théâtre et politique à la fin du Moyen Âge. Les entrées royales et autres cérémonies: mises au point et nouveaux aperçus', *Théâtre et spectacle hier et aujourd'hui, Moyen Âge et Renaissance. Actes du 115e congrès national des sociétés savantes* (Paris, 1991), p. 187.

erents: the whole city as a community of inhabitants, but also more specifically the mayor and aldermen who organized the entry, and lastly the actors, artists and craftsmen who put this entity into images and words. Of course, we have to assume that this character represents these three types of referents at the same time, but in each case the message conveyed is slightly different, as will be seen later. Likewise, the public is not a whole: according to the goal of the ceremony, the first receiver is Eleanor, and her suite, including the children of Francis I, hence the heirs to the throne. But the message is also implicitly addressed to the king, although he is not present, since he will most certainly be told by his wife and his suite what the plays performed at Eleanor's entry were. On the other hand, the message is also, although not directly, addressed to the citizens and inhabitants of Abbeville, since they are also present. To summarize, the message conveyed contains explicitly two types of subjects: first to Eleanor and through her, to the king, a praise of the royal couple and the allegiance to the king and hence to his new wife (addressed by Abbeville as a community of citizens and inhabitants) (l. 26-40 and 67-87), and also an appeal to free the prisoners, addressed rather by the officials of the city (l. 229-255); then, to the whole audience (addressed by the aldermen and the actors and artists), the explanation of the meaning of the next plays, although this explanation seems to be fully addressed to the royal couple and their suite (l. 90-94). However, this message may also contain implicitly other subjects, for instance if we consider that the aldermen invite the whole audience to enjoy themselves and to take pleasure in these plays. There might perhaps also be a message addressed to the citizens of Abbeville by the aldermen to render thus account of how they use the public finances to please the king and queen and how they serve the city by giving it a good reputation.

Thus, we see that the scheme of communication becomes more complex according to the way we interpret the speech of the characters on stage. The fact that the way chosen to convey this message is a dialogue staging allegories that are also real members of the audience makes it even more complicated. Indeed, there is a striking distancing effect since the character addresses the other characters and at the same time the person it represents and who is present in the audience. Thus, we can infer that the character of Abbeville addresses the king and the queen on stage, but also the queen in the audience, when she claims her loyalty, gives the explanation of the mystery plays, and asks Eleanor to free the prisoners. From a theatrical point of view, it is unclear how the characters are placed on stage: must we assume that the character turns towards the queen on the stage or towards the queen in the audience? To imagine the ways of staging such a play also reveals another level of communication, expressed through the exchanges of glances. Indeed, if the queen and her suite look mainly at the stages and decorations of the city, one can imagine that the inhabitants of Abbeville look as much at her as at the spectacle. George Chastelain describes this phenomenon in his *Chronique* when the Duke of Burgundy enters Paris in August 1471 to make sure everything is ready to welcome Louis XI. People of Paris, 'entre les mystères préparés de longue main, tendirent toutes les rues de riches draps, de tapisseries et d'autres jolivetés moult belles'.[8] however, when the Duke enters the city, he and his suite are so richly dressed that the attention of the people is drifted away from the decorations and the stages in his direction: when the Duke passes by,

> 'là où de peuple avoit tant haut et bas, et des dames aux fenestres que le nombre en fut inestimable, [...] s'esblouissoient les yeux des dames et des regardans sur les richesses et beauté de ceste compagnie. Et tant furent esmerveilliés et espris de joye, que à peine les bouches ne leur souffroient à vuydier par paroles ce que les yeux leur faisoient comprendre superflues et d'admiration dignes'.[9]

In fact, the words used to describe the reaction of the audience are exactly the same as those that would be used in case of a very striking dramatic performance. The sovereign and his or her suite become a spectacle for the people of the city, as interesting and magnificent as the spectacles prepared for them. Thus, just as the characters on stage can turn both towards each other and towards the public, the public of the city probably turns towards both the stage and the queen.

The three messages conveyed by the play, namely to express the loyalty of Abbeville towards the king, to explain the meaning of the short plays, and to ask the queen to free the prisoners, are also not as plain as it seems. Indeed, although the messages seem to be addressed to the queen, we realise that, eventually, they are addressed to the king, who is the real target. The message addressed to the queen is overtaken by the message addressed to a king who is not even present at that moment. Rather than to contemplate the possibility of a failure of symbolic communication – that would miss its real aim –, we should consider that the whole audience here: the queen, her suite, the aldermen and the rest of the population, know that they are them-

---

8. '*between the plays prepared long beforehand, [the people of Paris] stretched in every street rich draperies, tapestries and other very nice things*': Kervyn de Lettenhove, ed., *Œuvres de Georges Chastellain*, 8 vols. (Brussels, 1863-66), 4: 76.

9. '*where there were so many people above and below, and so many ladies at the windows that one could not count them, '...] the eyes of the ladies and of the other people were dazzled by the richness and the beauty of this company. And they were so amazed and delighted that their mouth was not able to express in superfluous words what their eyes revealed as deserving their admiration*': Kervyn de Lettenhove, ed., *op. cit.*, 4:77.

selves a medium to convey a part of the message to the king. Therefore, this diverted message is not confusing: the queen is certainly aware of the fact that her entry is also a good occasion for the people of Abbeville to sumptuously celebrate the entry of Francis I, although they are not supposed to do so, since the king has already entered officially the city. Then, it is quite normal that only a part of the play concerns her directly, and we can expect here that the audience perceives well the first degree of symbolic communication, that is to say the welcoming ceremony in honour of the queen, as well as its second degree, that is to say the symbolic welcoming of the king. In fact, the play builds up an ideal mirror or double of the event: it is a summary of the ideal course of the entry (if the king was taking part in it and enjoying it, and if the queen agreed to free the prisoners), and this mirror rests on the content of the dialogue as well as on the presence on stage of characters that are the doubles of the king and queen.

However, this way of conveying the request of the city to free the prisoners to the queen and implicitly to the king may seem unusual. Indeed, the aldermen decide here to represent the city itself and the royal couple on stage, and to put into the mouth of the characters the questions and answers, in short to let them dictate what the queen should reply to their request. Is there any danger in the idea of staging the royal couple in front of the eyes of the queen and the eyes of their relatives, who can inform the king precisely on the content of the play?

Staging the person of the king is common in royal entries, especially at the time of Francis I. It was customary then to put on stage a character representing the city as well as a character that represents the king surrounded by the royal symbols and attributes.[10] However, if it was not unusual for the allegory of the city to deliver a fairly long speech to the character of the king on stage or to the real king in the audience, it seems that the character of the king utters very seldom a long speech, except to praise the city in a very conventional way. For the entry of Charles VIII in Abbeville in 1493, a dialogue between Le Chef Souverain, Abbeville and Bon Désir had already been played. However, if we consult the text of the play, whose content we know thanks to the edition Alcius Ledieu made of the otherwise destroyed archives,[11] it was indeed such a predictable play where the city greets the king and the king praises the city in return. As Christian de Mérindol underlines, this play also presents the request of freeing the prisoners:

10. Anne-Marie Lecoq, *François Ier imaginaire* (Paris, 1987), pp. 369-375, and Christian de Mérindol, *op. cit.*, pp. 184-185.

11. See Christian de Mérindol, *op. cit.* and Alcius Ledieu, 'Première entrée de Charles VIII à Abbeville', *Bulletin Archéologique du Comité des travaux historiques* (1888), pp. 55-65.

'Dans le programme des entrées, des demandes précises sont parfois illustrées. Ainsi, à Abbeville, en 1493, la délivrance des prisonniers, le don de
la vue aux aveugles et la protection sont illustrées par une multitude de prisonniers voyants ou aveugles au pied de la Vierge'.[12]

The register describing the entry edited by Ledieu, evokes this scaffold:

'Pour le quart hourt, avoit une puchelle richement atournée, laquelle, tenant
en une de ses mains une paire de clefz richement faites, à l'aultre main ung
flambeau de vierge cire ardant; au dessoubz de laquelle Vierge estoit une
multitude de prisonniers, les ungz véans et les autres aveuglez. Et estoit le
tableau de ce hourt escript en teste: *Solve vincla reis*, et, au dessoubz, en
franchois:

Aux prisonniers deslie leurs loyens;
Aux aveuglez restitue lumière;
Garde le Roy de tous maux terriens;
Requiers qu'il ayt par toy grace plainière'.[13]

In the play explaining the meaning of the different 'tableaux vivants',
Bon Désir indeed asks the king to free the prisoners:

'Comme, par humblement requerre,
La Vierge, clémente et piteuse,
Prisonniers deslie et desserre,
De chartre obscure et ténébreuse,
Le Chief poeult hoster ses suppos,
Et, par la belle paix eureuse,
Donner lumière de reppos.[14]

However, this request is presented in a different way than in the *Declaracion*: this is a real question asked to the king through Bon Désir, whereas
in our play, Abbeville says the words she would like the queen to repeat,
and we can see that the Dame Souveraine already agrees on stage to free
the prisoners, as a logical consequence of the fulfilment of Psalm 22's end:

'Jesus me doint perseverance
D'avoir misericorde au coeur,
Et la preferer à rigueur
De justice en lieu et temps'. (l. 252-255)

---

12. Christian de Mérindol, *op. cit.*, p. 197.
13. '*for the fourth scaffold, there was a very richly adorned young girl who held in one
hand a pair of richly made keys, and in the other hand a glowing torch made of virgin wax;
under the aforesaid Virgin were a lot of prisoners, some who could see and some blind. And
on the sign of this scaffold was written "Solve vincla reis" and under it, in French: Untie
the chains of the prisoners, / Give back light to the blinds, / Keep the King away from all
earthly diseases, / Ask for him the entire grace*': Alcius Ledieu, *op. cit.*, p. 58.
14. '*As, when asked huymbly, / The Virgin, forgiving and merciful, / Unties and frees
the prisoners, / From a dark and murky gaol / The Chief can take his subjects / And, with
beautiful and joyful peace, / Give them the light of rest*': *Ibid.*, pp. 62-63.

The request of 1531 appears bolder than the request of 1493, since it already expects that the queen will reply in a positive way to it, by inducting through the whole play and the use of the Psalm an internal logic that leads only to a positive answer to the question.

As for this special request of freeing the prisoners, we have another instance of a play dealing with the same topic. It is a text published in the *Recueil de Poésies françoises des XVe et XVIe siècles* by Rothschild and Montaiglon, which stages the prisoners of the Châtelet, in Paris, for the entry of Eleanor in the city in 1530.[15] Like our *Declaracion*, it stages the request of freeing the prisoners, taking up the structure of the *Venite* of Psalm 94 and the comparison of the queen with the Virgin Mary ('*Venite*, l'estoille marine', l. 73). However, this text, although presented on a scene during the royal entry, is a poem presenting a petition and not a dialogue pregnant with real dramatic tension. Moreover, it asks the favour without postulating that it will be granted, and the royal couple does not appear on stage. There is a strict separation of roles, between those who ask humbly a favour, and the king and queen who listen to them but do not give any reply yet, this time coming later, but not during the entry.

I would like now to study briefly few other interesting instances from more or less the same period where the figure of a king is represented on stage in an unexpected situation, in order to see if we can find a compa-

---

15. Anatole de Montaiglon and James de Rothschild, *Recueil de Poésies françoises des XVe et XVIe siècles*, 13 vols. (Paris, 1876), 11: 253-276.
This poem, made of 20 stanzas, is called *Le Venite des Prisonniers du Chastelet de Paris sur la très-desirée entrée de la Royne de France*, and combine christian references to the Bible, particularly Psalm 94, *Venite Exultemus*, on wich lies the structure of the poem, with greek and latin mythology. Here is the second stanza which exposes the request of the prisoners:

Venite, l'Aigle Impérialle,
La très noble espouse royalle,
Venite, las ne tardez plus;
Venite, faconde nymphalle,
De paix l'auctrice très loyalle
Et des Roynes la par dessus.
Venite, ne faictes reffus
Des povres prisonniers confuz,
De toute liberté bannys;
Nous avons mys nostre espoir sus
Que à vostre entrée, sans nul abuz,
De prison serons eslargis.

[*Venite, imperial eagle, / Very noble royal spouse, / Venite, alas do not wait; / Venite, eloquent nymph, / The very loyal creator of peace / And among queens the one who is above. / Venite, do not refuse / The poor and ashamed prisoners, / Banned from all freedom; / We have put our hope above / That at your entry, without abuse / From our prison we will be freed.*]

For the entry of Eleanor in Paris and other parisian entries, see Lawrence M. Bryant, *The King and the City in the Parisian Royal Entry Ceremony: Politics, Ritual and Art in the Renaissance* (Genève, 1986).

rable type of situation, where the author of a play steps aside from the traditional way of representing the king and his speech on stage, to venture on to a more personal discourse. Jelle Koopmans pointed out to me the case of a play in Paris, in 1500, where Louis XII is represented as being ill, pale, his head wrapped with bandages and his feet in slippers.[16] We do not know the context in which this play may have been played, but it may certainly have been an instance of the staging of the king in an unconventional and non-traditional situation where the author puts his own words in the king's mouth, rather than restricting himself to the official line recommended if one represents a prince on stage. However, it is very likely that the author of this play had a satirical intention in mind, and that this play was staged unofficially or even secretly, to avoid the ire of the king, whereas the *Declaracion* was stage for a highly official occasion, and not at all in a satirical intention.

One can also think of the *Paix de Péronne*, by George Chastelain,[17] where Louis XI and Charles the Bold have a long dialogue about the peace they just concluded, a play that is likely to have been represented in front of the two monarchs. It could indeed be an example of a problematic staging of Princes, since, as Estelle Doudet underlines in her *thèse de doctorat*, the characters reflect in their dialogue, in veiled words, the point of view of Chastelain, who thinks this peace is not going to last:

> 'En rédigeant cette pièce de louange pour une paix récente, Chastelain, lucide observateur de son temps, sait que les deux adversaires d'hier, le roi de France et le duc de Bourgogne, ne signent qu'un accord mensonger. [...] Les personnifications de la *paix de Péronne*, se vidant elles-mêmes de leur sens, sont des indices du piège. Le dialogue devient tautologie, le hiératisme allégorique se fige dans un faux débat. L'interprétation des paroles échangées par Louis et Charles est laissée à des allégories méfiantes. [*The character*] Avis appelle à la subtilité d'interprétation et d'écriture, ce qui est peut-être un geste discret envers le lecteur'.[18]

This could indeed be another example where the character of the king is used to express the thoughts of the author. However, this dialogue is

---

16. Bernard Quilliet, *Louis XII, père du peuple* (Paris, 1986), p. 344: 'Dans l'une [des farces et sotties jouées], Louis XII était – comme par hasard – représenté malade, hâve, pâle, la tête enveloppé de pansements, les pieds dans des pantoufles; pour sa guérison, il demandait un brod d' "or potable", image un peu lourde (...). Dans une autre, convoquée par mère Sotte, une assemblée de Sotz Fieffez égratignait successivement tous les souverains de la chrétienté et désignait le roi de France comme le prince le plus avare de l'univers.'

17. Kervyn de Lettenhove, ed., *op.cit.*, 7: 423-452.

18. Estelle Doudet, *Poétique de Georges Chastelain*. Thèse de doctorat, Paris, La Sorbonne, pp. 69-70.

also at first sight quite innocuous even if it is always tinged with *double entendre*. The first level of reading presents a very conventional dialogue between two rulers on the verge of burying the hatchet, and it is only when we know the opinion of Chastelain on this event that we can read it as a hollow and somehow hypocritical dialogue on peace. The sovereigns and the audience are thus free not to hear Chastelain's allusions and to confine themselves to the first level that emphasizes the celebration of the peace agreement.

Therefore, from the texts I know and which were indicated to me, we are with the *Declaracion* in front of a slightly different case, where the message delivered in an official and very formal situation may be surprising for the royal audience, even slightly disturbing, since the royal couple is strongly incited to reply positively to the request of Abbeville, on grounds of following the precepts exposed in Psalm 22 in order to be a good Christian:

'Je doibz faire misericorde
A ceulx que prison advironne.
Par cest oeuvre, j'ay esperance
D'habiter en la maison Dieu' (l. 246-249)

From what we know from the registers of the city, it seems however that this play did not raised any extraordinary reaction from the queen and her suite, or from the king at a later stage. The accounting books record that the king stayed in the city for three weeks and seemed to fully enjoy his visit. What may seem to us now an audacious message conveyed to the king has apparently been well perceived by him.

If we consider this text in the light of the rituals displayed in royal entries at the time, we realise that its problematic way of expressing a request nevertheless fits into the scheme of communication of *sacra*. Jesse Hurlbut applies the following ethnological observation developed by Victor and Edith Turner to the civic entries of the Duke of Burgundy;[19] the royal entry turns into a religious celebration, and thus performs the same kind of rituals as in other celebrations that belong to the same category. One of the essential aspects is the communication of *sacra*, that is to say 'sacred things' from the Latin terms, these being either objects or concepts; this communication may be performed by exhibition, by delivering instructions or by actions. The latter especially can consist of 'dra-

19. Jesse D. Hurlbut, 'The Duke's First Entry: Burgundian Inauguration and Gift', *Moving Subjects. Processional Performance in the Middle Ages and the Renaissance* (Amsterdam, 2001), pp. 155-185; Victor and Edith Turner, 'Religious Celebration', *Celebration: Studies in Festivity and Ritual* (Washington, 1982), pp. 201-219.

matic performances'.[20] Here would be one reason why the *Declaracion* takes its structure from a psalm, in order to underline its religious dimension. According to Hurlbut,

> 'The more elaborate expressions of the *sacra* (all generated by the city) allowed the city to establish a form of potentially profitable discourse with the duke, in the name of the ritual initiation of their relationship. Although the city was not in a hierarchical position to teach the duke his responsibilities, it could, nevertheless, hope that a carefully orchestrated presentation of the idealized political relationship (through a development of the *sacra*) would capture the duke's attention, if only on the level of suggestion.'[21]

In our *Declaracion*, this idealised political relationship is presented on stage through the mutual respect and esteem between the royal couple and Abbeville: the Seigneur Souverain praises Abbeville, 'beaucoup famée, / Et de nous grandement amée,' (l. 56-57), and Abbeville repeats her allegiance to him, saying: 'Possede moy, tu es mon Roy, / Je soustiendray tout ton arroy, / Obeissant à ta personne' (l. 74-76).

Moreover, this ritual dimension explains why the city may feel allowed to present its request on stage, in a dramatic performance, and in a rather informal tone:

> 'The production of highly connotative stage performances gave the city an invaluable opportunity to express its concerns and to produce messages containing the models of and for the city, the duke, and their relationship. By assuming the communication of the *sacra,* the city could manipulate this discourse between the two parties in the exchange. By emphasizing the duke's power and the city's worthiness, ceremony organizers not only guided the foundation of the political relationship, but also raised the duke, the city, and the bond between the two to a cultural level of identification.'[22]

In this context, what would usually seem a bold message addressed to the royal authority becomes a request delivered in an unusual but admissible way.

To sum up, we are here confronted with a case where tradition in the treatment of symbolic communication is very strong, but where the event leads to a rather new way of staging the royal figures, especially the king, and to new ways to address the royal couple. Indeed, the whole ceremony follows a very set order, with greetings to the queen, plays performed and gifts offered: the very same order that was in use in the pre-

20. Hurlbut, *op. cit.*, p. 159.
21. Ibidem, p. 175.
22. Id, p. 175.

vious century, and which remains unchanged to a certain extent in northern France and in Flanders until the end of the 16th century. The different steps of the preparation in the registers insist on the importance of following the usual procedure, as is generally the case for royal entries. The main sentence that comes in such case is 'to do as usual' ('comme à l'acoustumée'), and this expression does not merely imply that nothing needs to change in the ceremony but also that nothing *must* change.

Since the city council wants to follow strictly the tradition set in the case of a royal entry, it cannot offer the king a sumptuous entry, for the reasons already evoked. But, to celebrate this exceptional event: the king coming back to the city after a long time, the city can still make use of the welcoming plays, which can express the deference of the inhabitants and citizens of Abbeville. Thus, Abbeville transforms the usual system of the symbolic communication in a royal entry by greeting more an absent king than a present queen. We can even advance the idea that this king on stage is in some way a double of the real king who cannot be here, that the king as a character replaces the absent king. In the context of celebrating the arrival of the king, this somewhat diverted communication apparently seemed very understandable and natural to the audience.

Moreover, the traditional type of play performed in such occasion is to some extent modified by the way the customary request of freeing the prisoners of the city is presented. But again, the audience, including the queen herself, are not disturbed to see the characters on stage speak freely in front of the queen about what she should do. This has to do, in my opinion, with the fact that the traditional ceremony is otherwise scrupulously observed, and that, in its religious as well as civic aspects, it complies with the respective duties of subjects toward their king and of a king toward his subjects.

Why was the play written down in the city's register of deliberation, not a place where one would expect to find the text of a play, since the plays, if ever they were kept, were usually written down on separate manuscripts? We have no definitive answer to this question. However, this decision of the city council tends to prove that, for its members, it was important and worth being saved, just as the text of the play performed for the first entry of Charles VIII, in the same place, almost forty years earlier, had been judged worth being kept in this register too. Does it come from a local tradition of conservation of this type of play or from a wish to be able to re-use the texts for another occasion? These considerations have probably played a part. But such a play might also have been kept in order to remember a singular and inventive way of following an old tradition, at a moment when one begins to take an interest in the new topics and themes of the coming Renaissance. This is precisely such a step that can be interesting in regard of symbolic communication, when theatre brings up new ways of following old paths.

Universiteit van Amsterdam - NWO

Appendix

Play performed for the entry of Eleanor of Habsburg in Abbeville Municipal archives of Abbeville; registre aux délibérations de l'échevinage, BB, 63, fol. 135 v° sqq (destroyed).

I reproduce the edition of Ledieu, with his own notes. I brought no changes to it, except the quotation marks l.244-251, to make clearly appear that Abbeville quotes here what the queen should say as a conclusion of the interpretation of Psalm 22.

La declaracion des misteres faictz à l'entrée de la tres noble et excellente dame et Royne de France madame Alyenor.

Le Seigneur Souverain

C'est merveilles de Piramus
Qui, de mort, alloit degoyser
Soubz le meurier comme la mus,
Il debvoit Thisbes espouser.

La Dame souveraine

Mariage cler que Phebus   5
Ordonne de Dieu droicturier,
Ne cherche nocturnaulx abus,
On s'y peust bien aparier.

Le Seigneur souverain

Soubz le meurier et la fontaine,
Piramus deceupt se deffit.   10
De son corps pareil murdre fit,
Thisbes, dame noble et haultaine.

La Dame

Hypocrisie de dol plaine,
Quy le coeur obtenebre et nuict,

Feit apparoistre que la nuict, 15
De peché rend l'ame vilaine.

Le Seigneur

Le meurier changea sa coulleur
En fruict rouge et sanguinollent;
Comme triste et du cas dollent,
A tousjours porté la doulleur. 20

La Dame

L'arbre[23] de soy meilleur,
Que le meurier et excellent,
Ne change du fruict opullent,
Car il est constant en valleur.

Le Seigneur

De malefice vient malleur. 25

La Dame

De bonté procede tout bien.
Mon cher seigneur, nous povons bien,
En conjugale honnesteté,
Neantmoins qu'il ne soit osté,
Nous transporter vers nos amys 30
Et subgectz, lesquelz Dieu a mys
Soubz vostre souveraine forche.

Le Seigneur

Ad ce faire, mon voeul s'efforche,
Non point pour gloire acumuler,
Mais pour voir et dissimuler 35
Toutes choses à mon possible.
Dieu merchis! mon regne est paisible:
On me ayme, on me crainct et doubte,
Dont sans suspineuse doubte,
Monstrer me doibz à mes suppotz. 40

La Dame

En enssuivant vostre propos,
Pour avoir recreacion,

23. Blanc

La nostre congregacion,
Transportons en la Picardie.

　　　Le Seigneur

Ne doubtez que je contredie   45
A vostre requeste, ma doulce:
Je vous advise bien de bouche
Que une vallée vous verrez,
Où soullas vous percheverez,
Plus largement que ne vous somme.   50

　　　La Dame

Son nom?

　　　Le Seigneur

　　　La vallée de Somme.
Ung lieu delicat, fructueulx,
Gouverné de gentz vertueulx,
Et leaulx à vostre regence;
Veu vous avez à diligence   55
Abbeville beaucoup famée,
Et de nous grandement amée,
Toute prompte à gendarmerie,
Donner grandz coups d'artillerye,
Nous recepvant en ses attours;   60
Elle ne a ne chasteau ne tours,
Que pour nous n'ayt toujours gardé
Et songneusement regardé
A tout comme france et fidelle.

　　　La Dame

A bon droict dict grand bien d'elle;   65
Regardez, elle vous salue.

　　　Abbeville

Tres cher Roy de value[24],
Plus preux que Hector de Priam filz[25];
Tous mes désirs sont assaissis
Quant ta personne je regarde;   70
Tu es ma seulle sauvegarde

24. Il manque deux pieds.
25. Il y a un pied en trop.

Aprez Dieu et les benoistz sainctz;
Mes Abbevillois te sont sains;
Possede moy, tu es mon Roy,
Je soustiendray tout ton arroy,   75
Obeissant à ta personne.

    La Dame

Son voulloir au vostre consonne;
Ma foy, voylà noble picarde.

    Abbeville

Madame, quant je vous regarde,
Mon coeur se pasme; neantmoins,   80
Vous saluant à joinctes mains,
Genoulx flexis et d'humble chère,
Je vous prie faire grande chère
En vos limites dont j'ai nice,
Car tout mon courage pronice   85
A vous rescreer sus ma foy
Que faict la serve pour sa dame.

    La Dame

Sy ne me aymiez de corps et de ame,
Vous n'eussiez faict telz appareulx;
Vos misteres, quy n'ont pareulx,   90
Me plaisent fort et me rescréent;
Mais dictes-moy sy vous aggrée
La substance, et ne faillez point.

    Abbeville

Madame, pour le premier point,
La fontaine au prez du verger   95
Seignifie, pour abregier,
L'eaue de Somme doulce et profonde,
Laquelle son cours maine et fonde
Environ le verger plaisant,
Lequel nous sommes exposant   100
Le royaulme tres crestien,
Où le Roy et vous je soubstien,
Triumphans en estat royal,
Dont moy mesmes, de coeur loyal,
L'Eglise, bourgois et gentilz,   105
Avons, comme promptz et actis,
Ledict mistere, à vostre entrée,

Extraict de la lettre sacrée
Du pseaultier hault estimé
Qu'on dit: *Dominus regit me*;   110
Et est la lettre toute telle
Que vous me orrez dise escoutelle
Le tres crestien Roy François;
Monseigneur me conduict et maine
En Abbeville, doulce et humaine,   115
Où trouverray lieu à mon choix
Dessus l'eaue de reffection,
Et au verger de son royaulme
Il a seul converty mon ame,
A sa grande dellectation.   120

          Le Seigneur

Voilà belle exposicion
Et fondée en la vérité.

          La Dame

Je vous donne l'auctorité
De parachever.

          Le Seigneur

     Il le faut.

     Abbeville

En nostre second eschaffault,   125
Estoit le Roy soubz sainct Michiel.
Signant que Dieu transmist du ciel
A ses ancestres l'armarie
De France sus toute cherie.
En aprez, le Roy sans ensonne,   130
Presentant à vostre personne
L'agneau d'or, faict seignifiance
Qu'en vous en tout mist sa fiance,
Nous alliant en seure paix,
Dont justice par ses aspectz   135
Confute belliqueuse esclandre;
Ad ce propos, la salemandre,
Par son povoir quy poinct et picque,
Reboute la guerre et la picque
De la tres hideuse Atropos.   140

Le Seigneur

Donnez-nous de cela l'expos
Sus *Deduxit me*[26] contenu,
Et que sens y soit mainctenu.

Abbeville

Par allyance et foy promise,
Qui sont de justice sentiers,   145
M'ont ycy deduict vollentiers
Pour son hault nom m'y suis submise;
La guerre et umbrage de mort
Sont enversés et mis au bas;
Je ne doubteray leurs combas,   150
Car la sallemandre les mort.

La Dame

Voylà bien dict.

Le Seigneur

Sans mal remord,
On n'y sçauroit que repplicquer.

Abbeville

Je vous le diray à bref plet.
Le Roy assis, sceptre tenant,   155
Denote qu'il est gouvernant
Son royaume à commandement,
Et n'est sy osé vrayement
Quy ne tremble soubz son baston.
Par son espée congnoist on   160
Qu'il faict justice à tout endroict,
En punissant selon le droict
Ses subgectz quand ilz ont mespris
Ses trois nobles filz bien apris,
Vrais fleurons du lis pululans,   165
Au Roy et à ses biens voeulans
Donnent tres grande esjouissance,
Car ilz renfforchent la puissance
Du royaume en telle maniere
Qu'ilz deffenderont la baniere   170
De France, s'on l'esvahissoit,

26. Ps. XXII, v. 3.

Dont mon poeuple s'esjouissoit
A vostre advenue nouvelle.

La Dame

J'entends le cas.

Le Seigneur

    Qu'on nous revelle
En substance sans tarder plus   175
Virga tua, et baculus[27].

Abbeville

Ta verge de direction
Et tres illustre geniture,
De ton sceptre la florature
Me donnent consollation.   180
Abbeville en Ponthieu lealle,
A ma venue faict grand chere;
J'en tiendray sa nation chere,
Qui ne fust oncques desleale.

Le Seigneur

L'application n'est pas male,   185
Vostre propos suit à plaisir.

La Dame

Abbeville, prenez loisir
A nous déclarer le iiij^e.

Abbeville

Le Roy, assis en son lieu sublime,
Du Sainct Esprit advironné,   190
Note que Dieu luy a donné
Pour regir ce royaume insigne
Une unction et sacré signe
Que n'ont aultres roys crestiens;
Car je voeulx dire et sy soustiens   195
Que, moyennant la saincte ampole,
Dont il est oingt seul soubz le pole,
Les escroelles il efface,

27. Ps. XXII, v. 4.

Par ung singulier don de grace;
Et, à la raison que madame,   200
Sa tres eureuse espouse et femme,
A luy par mariage unit,
Il s'enssuit que Dieu la munit
De benediction pareille;
La doulce boisson non pareille,   205
Dont le Roy present luy a faict,
Et qu'elle a savouré de faict,
C'est l'honneur, la joye et triumphe
Qu'elle a, puis que, avecq luy triumphe
Par tout le royaume de France.   210
Les douze pers font demonstrance
Que, pour le Roy magnifier,
Ilz ont voullu ratiffier
Leur Royne en luy faisant service.

        La Dame

Impiguasti[28], voullentiers veisse   215
Mis en françois; parlez à tant,
Comme le bref le fut portant.

        Abbeville

Ton chef est oinct du sacré sacre;
Toy et moy ne sommes que ung corps,
En mariage ainsy concordz;   220
Ton chef sacré le mien consacre;
O que tres cler est mon calice,
Auquel mon Roy et mon seigneur
M'abruve du royal honneur,
Melliflueux et sans malice!   225

        Le Seigneur

Enssuivant vostre proposé,
Cestui vers est bien exposé.
Que le dernier nous soit decis.

        Abbeville

Le Roy en majesté assis,
Qui faisoit signe d'une verge,   230
A la Royne luy donnant cherge,
En son haultain royal povoir,

28. Ps. XXII, v. 5.

Hors des prisons leur donnant grace,
Ce qu'elle a faict en ceste place, 235
A son joyeulx advenement,
Esperant par foy tellement
Parvenir en l'eternel regne,
Où nostre Dieu qui, tousjours regne,
Intronise ses bons amis. 240

La Dame

Exposés comment avez mys
En françois le final dictier?

Le Seigneur

Dictes, je l'orray voullentiers.

Abbeville

"Puisque je porte la couronne,
Et que droict royal le m'accord, 245
Je doibz faire misericorde
A ceulx que prison advironne.
Par cest oeuvre, j'ay esperance
D'habiter en la maison Dieu,
Lequel par foy m'y donra lieu 250
De perpetuelle asseurance."

La Dame

Jesus me doint perseverance
D'avoir misericorde au coeur,
Et la preferer à rigueur
De justice en lieu et temps. 255

Le Seigneur

Nous sommes de vous tres contens,
Abbeville, je vous afferme.

Abbeville

Pour fin, je crieray de voix ferme:
Dieu gard de mal et de royne
Le Roy François et la Royne, 260
Le daulfin avecq ses deux freres!
Aiez prins en gré nos misteres.

Finis.

Jacoba VAN LEEUWEN

BALANCING TRADITION AND RITES OF REBELLION: THE RITUAL TRANSFER OF POWER IN BRUGES ON 12 FEBRUARY 1488[1]

In late medieval Flemish towns a new municipality was elected and installed yearly. This ritual transfer was a statutory act of great political importance, since it had to demonstrate the legal foundations of power in the town. Recent research has dealt with this ritual in Hanseatic, French, Italian and Swiss towns.[2] In his study on urban norms and values, Isenmann has underlined the importance of this ritual in urban life, when he

---

1. This article is based on my PhD: *De Vlaamse wetsvernieuwing. Een onderzoek naar de jaarlijkse keuze en aanstelling van het stadsbestuur in Gent, Brugge en Ieper in de Middeleeuwen,* Verhandelingen van de Koninklijke Vlaamse Academie van België voor Wetenschappen en Kunsten, Nieuwe reeks, 15 (Brussels, 2004), pp. 178-187. I thank the 'Bijzonder Onderzoeksfonds of the K.U. Leuven' for giving me the opportunity to rework my findings. I also thank prof. D. Money for helping me with the English translation and J. Haemers for his comments upon an earlier version of this text.

2. Germany: D.W. Poeck, 'Zahl, Tag und Stuhl. Zur Semiotik der Ratswahl', *Frühmittelalterliche Studien,* 33 (1999), pp. 396-427; D.W. Poeck, 'Rituale der Ratswahl in westfälischen Städten', *Vormoderne politische Verfahren. Zeitschrift für historische Forschung, Beiheft,* 25 (2001), pp. 207-262; J. Rogge, 'Ir freye wale zu haben. Möglichkeiten, Probleme und Grenzen der politischen Partizipation in Augsburg zur Zeit der Zunftverfassung (1368-1548)', in *Stadtregiment und Bürgerfreiheit. Handlungsspielräume in deutschen und italienischen Städten des Späten Mittelalters und der Frühen Neuzeit,* eds. K. Schreiner and U. Meier, Bürgertum. Beiträge zur europäischen Gesellschaftsgeschichte, 7 (Göttingen, 1994), pp. 244-277.

Italy: H. Keller, '"Kommune": Städtische Selbstregierung und mittelalterliche "Volksherrschaft" im Spiegel italienischer Wahlverfahren des 12.-14. Jahrhunderts', in *Person und Gemeinschaft im Mittelalter. Karl Schmid zum 65 Geburtstag,* ed. G. Althoff (Sigmaringen, 1988), pp. 573-616; Idem, 'Wahlformen und Gemeinschaftsverständnis in den Italienischen Stadtkommunen 12./14. Jahrhunderts. Voraussetzungen und Wandlungen', in *Wahlen und Wählen im Mittelalter,* eds. R. Schneider and H. Zimmermann, Vorträge und Forschungen. Herausgegeben vom Konstanzer Arbeitskreis für mittelalterliche Geschichte, 37 (Sigmaringen, 1990), pp. 345-374.

Switserland: R. Schmid, 'Wahlen in Bern. Das Regiment und seine Erneuerung im 15. Jahrhundert', *Berner Zeitschrift für Geschichte und Heimatkunde,* 58 (1996), pp. 233-270. France: A. Rigaudière, 'Voter dans les villes de France au Moyen Âge (XIIIe-XVe S.)', *Academie des inscriptions et belles lettres. Comptes rendus des séances,* 4 (2000), pp. 1439-1471; B. Chevalier, *Les bonnes villes de France du XIVe au XVIe siecle* (Paris, 1982), pp. 202-210.

stated that: 'the festivities celebrating the inauguration of a new council, were the most ostentatious and legally binding manifestation of the unity of the citenzenry'.[3] But the question as to how this transfer functioned in medieval Flanders still remained open. Moreover, the political and social context in this county differed significantly from other European towns. Flanders was one of the most urbanized areas of late medieval Europe and the independence of its towns was threatened by the centralizing efforts of its rulers, the Burgundian dukes. These rulers also wanted to leave their mark on the ritual just as much as the urban communities. Thus, the yearly ritual transfer played a key role in the relations between urban and ducal power. This yearly transfer of power within towns caused much debate and conflicts and thus several changes in the ritual system were made so that the ritual should mirror changes in the balance of power. Each time the new social position of the aldermen was communicated symbolically.

This contribution seeks to explore the changes the ritual election and installation of aldermen underwent during an imporant urban uprising in 1488. Recent research into the history of Flanders has demonstrated the importance of ritual behaviour during such urban uprisings. The rebellious crowd often expressed its political grievances with the elaboration of an alternative set of symbolic actions, often based on the appropriation of well known traditions.[4] Here, we would like to question if and how these 'rites of rebllion' have influenced the election and installation of a new bench of aldermen during the revolt of 1488. During this severe crisis the rebels required that a new municipality should be installed without inter-ference of the count. Thus, they were forced to elaborate their own rit-ual; they could not, however, ignore its tradition. How did they proceed?

3. E. Isenmann, 'Norms and Values in the European City', in *Resistance, Representa-tion and Community,* ed. P. Blickle, The Origins of the Modern State in Europe (Oxford, 1997), p. 196.

4. P. Arnade, 'Secular Charisma, Sacred Power: Rites of Rebellion in the Ghent Entry of 1467', *Handelingen der maatschappij voor geschiedenis en oudheidkunde te Gent, Nieuwe Reeks,* 45 (1991), pp. 69-94; Idem, 'Crowds, Banners, and the Marketplace: Symbols of Defiance and Defeat during the Ghent War of 1452-1453', *Journal of Medieval and Renais-sance Studies,* 24 (1994), pp. 471-497; J. Haemers, 'A moody community? Emotion and rit-ual in late medieval urban revolts', in *Emotions in the city (XIVth – XVIth centuries),* eds. E. Lecuppre-Desjardin and A.-L. Van Bruaene, Studies in European Urban History (1200-1800), 5 (Turnhout, 2005), pp. 63-81; J. Haemers and E. Lecuppre-Desjardin, 'Conquérir et reconquérir l'espace urbain. Le triomphe de la collectivité sur l'individu dans le cadre de la révolte Brugeoise de 1488', in *Groupes sociaux et territoires urbains du Moyen Âge au 16ᵉ siècle,* ed. C. Deligne (Turnhout, 2006); J. Dumolyn, '"Rebelheden ende vergaderingen". Twee Brugse documenten uit de grote opstand van 1436-1438', *Handelingen van de konin-klijke commissie voor geschiedenis,* 162 (1996), pp. 197-223.

Which strategies were followed to compose the ritual and why? Were these changes exceptional, or can we trace them in other urban revolts as well? Moreover, can we label them as typical rebellious interventions or did rulers also employ them? And, finally, did the rebels only change the margins of the ritual or was its solemn core also adapted?

1. The traditional ritual transfer in medieval Bruges

In the late Middle ages the municipality of Bruges consisted of twelve aldermen, twelve councillors and two mayors: one for each bench. The authority to choose and install the town's governors was a privilege of the count of Flanders. In theory this ruler was entitled to act on his own, but he usually sent deputies for this purpose. These representatives had to present a letter of delegation to the resigning aldermen in order to prove the legitimacy of their mandate.[5] In the latter part of the fourteenth century, these deputies chose the twelve aldermen and received their oath. Then, these aldermen retired to the council chamber and elected the councillors and the mayors. This scheme was used until 1399 when, after a conflict with the duke, it was arranged that the ducal deputies could propose candidates for the position of councillor and mayor. The new aldermen were only allowed to refuse these nominees in specific circumstances. Only in 1477, after the death of Charles the Bold, was this system abolished, and the town demanded that the older scenario was reinstated. Moreover, the seats of government were to be distributed among the nine members of the town's population who represented the burghers and the guilds. This scenario was in use until 1485 and probably later too.[6]

5. On these deputies: P. Van Peteghem, 'Het commissariaat voor de wetsvernieuwing en voor het afhoren van de rekeningen in Vlaanderen (14de-18de eeuw). Controle en beheersing van het eerst en meest geürbaniseerde gebied der Nederlanden', in *De Vlaamse instellingen tijdens het ancien régime: recent onderzoek in nieuw perspectief. Symposium georganiseerd te Brugge op 18 mei 1998,* eds. W. Prevenier and B. Augustyn, Miscellanea archivistica, Studia 91 (Brussel, 1999), p. 67-138; D. Clauzel, 'Le renouvellement de l'eschevinage à la fin du Moyen Age: l'exemple de Lille (1380-1500)', *Revue du Nord,* 77 (1995), 365-385.

6. D. Van den Auweele, *Schepenbank en schepenen te Brugge (1127-1384). Bijdrage tot de studie van een gewone stedelijke rechts- en bestuursinstelling,* Unpublished Phd, K.U.Leuven, 1977; J. Mertens, 'Bestuursinstellingen van de stad Brugge (1127-1795)', in: *De gewestelijke en lokale overheidsinstellingen in Vlaanderen tot 1795,* eds. W. Prevenier and B. Augustyn, Algemeen rijksarchief en Rijksarchief in de provinciën, Studia 72 (Brussels, 1997), pp. 323-332; K. Vanhaverbeke, 'De reële machtsstructuren binnen het stadsbestuur van Brugge in de periode 1375-1407. Verslag van een prosopografische studie', *Handelingen van het genootschap voor geschiedenis, gesticht onder de benaming 'Société d'émulation' te Brugge,* 134 (1998), pp. 3-54.

The ritual of election and installing a new municipality in Bruges was celebrated yearly with great solemnity on 2 September. In the fifteenth century this ritual was usually staged as follows. First, the great bell of the Belfry was rang so all the inhabitants of the town knew that the transfer of power had started. On this sign the ducal deputies and the resigning municipality went to St. Donatien's church where a mass for the Holy Spirit was celebrated. Here, it was prayed that divine grace would inspire the deputies. After this mass, the officials entered the town hall where representatives of the town's inhabitants had gathered. A clerk showed the letters of delegation to the public and read out the text. If necessary, he also translated these documents from French into Dutch. On the basis of these letters, the resigning aldermen then confirmed the official status of the ducal deputies. They also explicitly referred to the privileges and customs that bound the actions of the delegates. Thus, the audience was informed about the legal foundations of the election and it was demonstrated that the ducal deputies were legitimate. Moreover, this transparency of the proceedings facilitated control over the ritual. After this, the names of the new aldermen were proclaimed. The public was allowed to react and could ask for changes in the composition of this board. Of course, good arguments were needed to grant their request. After this proclamation the aldermen swore their oath publicly. Between 1477 and 1485 a conclave was held afterwards, followed by the proclamation and oath-taking of the councillors and mayors. The sources do not prove that this meeting took place after 1485, but there is no evidence of the opposite either.[7] After the official ceremony, banquets and other gatherings concluded the festivities.[8]

2. The revolt in Bruges: February 1488

In April 1482 Mary, Duchess of Burgundy, died unexpectedly. Immediately, a political vacuum came into existence in Flanders. The heir,

7. This traditional scenario is based on several sources. The *Registers van de wetsvernieuwingen* recorded yearly the composition of all the corporations in the town. Marginal notes give information about the ritual followed. [SAB, Oud archief, 114]. Town-accounts are also a valuable source [SAB, Oud archief, 216]. In 1398 the inhabitants of Bruges described their view of the ritual [ARA, Oorkonden van Vlaanderen, II, box 13, nr, 419]. For a later description, see: Joos de Damhouder, *De magnificentia politiae amplissimae civitatis Brugarum cum eiusdem topographia et in laudem amplissimi senatus oratione* (Antwerp, Johannis Bellerem, 1564), pp. 126 r-v.
8. About these festivities: J. van Leeuwen, 'Geluid, muziek en entertainment. Het gebruik van auditieve communicatiemiddelen tijdens het ritueel van de wetsvernieuwing in Gent, Brugge en Ieper (1379-1493)', *Belgisch tijdschrift voor filologie en geschiedenis* (in press).

Philip the Fair was a minor and could therefore not succeed yet. His father, Maximilian of Austria wanted to reign as his guardian and regent, but the county of Flanders offered much resistance. Maximilian's urge for centralization was the main problem. On 5 June 1483 the succession was finally arranged: a regency would rule the county of Flanders on behalf of Philip the Fair. This regency consisted of representatives of both the nobility and the towns. It was, amongst other competencies, authorized to select and install the benches of aldermen all over Flanders.[9] However, Maximilian did not acknowledge his defeat so easily: from 1484 onwards he waged war against the Flemish towns and in July 1485 he overthrew the regency. The towns were punished severely for their defiance. Moreover, Maximilian visited Ghent and Bruges personally; and in these towns he appointed a new municipality on his behalf. He restricted the town's autonomy and installed an authoritarian government.[10] His triumph was short-lived, since in November 1487 a new revolt broke out in Ghent. Thus they caused a severe crisis in the county.[11] The French king Charles VIII resolved to support the Flemish rebels.

From December 1487 onwards Maximilian resided in Bruges and negotiated with Ghent in order to restore the peace. Meanwhile, troops of Ghent marched to Bruges, thus alarming the ruler severely. Therefore, Maximilian wished to fortify Bruges with his own troops, towards the end of January. The Brugeans, however, put a stop to this plan and closed all the town's gates. Not much later, a revolt broke out. The guilds assembled armed on the market place and lined up under their banners. They demanded complete publicity in decision making and wished to be

9. J.M. Cauchies, *Philippe le Beau. Le dernier duc de Bourgogne*, Burgundica 6 (Turnhout, 2003), pp. 3-40; W.P. Blockmans, 'Autocratie ou polyarchie? La lutte pour le pouvoir politique en Flandre de 1482 à 1492, d'après des documents inédits', *Handelingen van de koninklijke commissie voor geschiedenis*, 140 (1974), pp. 257-368, comments: at 280; W.P. Blockmans, *De volksvertegenwoordiging in Vlaanderen in de overgang van Middeleeuwen naar Nieuwe Tijden (1384-1506)* (Brussels, 1978), pp. 314-15; R. van Uytven, 'Crisis als cesuur 1482-1494', in *Algemene geschiedenis der Nederlanden, 5* (Haarlem, 1980), 420-35 at 423; M. Boone, 'La justice en spectacle. La justice urbaine en Flandre et la crise du pouvoir «bourguignon» (1477-1488)', *Revue historique*, 127 (2003), pp. 43-65.

10. Blockmans, 'Autocratie', 291; W.P. Blockmans, 'Breuk of continuïteit? De Vlaamse privilegiën van 1477 in het licht van het Staatsvormingsproces', in W.P. Blockmans, ed., *Le privilège general et les privilèges regionaux de Marie de Bourgogne pour les Pays-Bas – 1477 – Het algemene en de gewestelijke privilegiën van Maria van Bourgondië voor de Nederlanden* (Kortrijk-Heule, 1985), pp. 97-144 at 116.

11. Ghent, municipal archives, Oud archief, Stadscharters 752 en 753. See also: V. Fris, 'Jan van Coppenhole', *Bulletijn der Maatschappij van geschied- en Oudheidkunde te Gent*, 14 (1906), pp. 93-114.

informed about the grievances Ghent had uttered on the rule of Maximilian. Moreover, they forbade this ruler to leave the town. On 3 February two of the town's officials were discharged and their successors were solemnly installed and took the oath of obedience to the county of Flanders and Philip the Fair. Two days later, Maximilian was imprisoned in a house located on the marketplace of Bruges. The Three Members (chief towns) of Flanders: Ghent, Bruges and Ypres, had seized power over the county. They wished to put a definite stop to the politics of centralization led by Maximilian and thus restore the towns' autonomy. Peace-negotiations started soon afterwards. Representatives of Ghent came to Bruges and took control over the town. They refused to negotiate with the aldermen in Bruges, since these officials were installed on behalf of Maximilian. Even though Bruges proposed that the municipality should swear a new oath, Ghent demanded that new aldermen, councillors and mayors should be elected and installed instead. Ghent was in charge of this exceptional ritual transfer of power, which took place on 12 February 1488.[12]

3. The ritual transfer of power on 12 February 1488

According to the town accounts of Bruges the ritual change of power on 12 February was not exceptional at all. Just like in the previous years, the bell-ringer of the belfry was rewarded to announce the start of the ritual publicly by tolling the town's bell.[13] According to the same source, official deputies attended the ritual as usual and received a fee for their services.[14] Expenses for the banquet after the elections are recorded too, just like every year.[15] Thus, these accounts suggest that, apart from the date, no other changes to the usual scenario were made. Nevertheless, the political context posed some problems, and so the rebels were obliged to adapt four components of the scenario: the initiative of the event, the ritual space, the oath-formulae and the composition of the municipality.

---

12. On this revolt, see: R. Wellens, 'La révolte Brugeoise de 1488', *Handelingen van het Genootschap voor Geschiedenis gesticht onder de benaming 'Société d'Emulation' te Brugge*, 102 (1965), pp. 5-52; A. Janssens, 'Macht en onmacht van de Brugse schepenbank in de periode 1477-1490', *Handelingen van het Genootschap voor Geschiedenis gesticht onder de benaming 'Société d'Emulation' te Brugge*, 133 (1996), pp. 5-45.

13. Bruges, municipal archives, Oud archief, 216, Stadsrekening 1488, fol. 130r.

14. Idem, fol. 142r.

15. Idem, rekening 1487-1488, fol. 124r.

3.1. The initiative of the transfer of power

In February 1488 the Ghent party took the initiative to replace the governors in Bruges, stating that the political context necessitated a power transfer. According to the town's privileges, the aldermen and councillors of Bruges could only be installed lawfully by the interference of legitimate countal deputies who could produce a letter of delegation. Ghent, however, stipulated that the new aldermen had to be installed on behalf of Philip the Fair: the true count of Flanders. Charles VIII, de French king, supported their ambitions by granting Ghent permission on 17 January 1488 to choose and install all the Flemish magistrates.[16] Thus, the power of the aldermen, councillors and mayors would still be based on a superior level of power.

Several sources mention that no letters of delegation were issued for the ritual on 12 February 1488; however, Ghent did send official delegates who acted as legitimate substitutes for the usual countal deputies. As sketched earlier, the solemn recognition of the status of these representatives formed an important component of the opening of the ritual. It could not be left out, since the legitimacy of the entire ritual was rooted in this action. Ghent had to respect this tradition and needed to find a way around the problem. Thus the rebels decided to publish the privilege granted to Ghent earlier at the start of the transfer of power. This document should demonstrate the legitimacy of their act and the legal foundation of the delegation.[17] Apparently, this caused no problems in Bruges and the legitimacy of the deputies was not questioned.

However, in doing so, Ghent did take a risk, since the consent of Bruges was not obvious. This is demonstrated by the reaction of Ypres in February 1488. The rebels also wished to replace the municipality in this town and referred to the privilege granted on 17 January in order to prove the lawfulness of their claim. The resigning aldermen of Ypres were however quite suspicious and demanded that the Ghent delegates should take the original document along with them so that it could be examined by the magistrates in Ypres. Ghent refused to do so, stating that the document was too valuable to transport trough a rebellious county.[18] Ypres then decided

16. Ghent, municipal archives, Oud archief, reeks 93, 7/G, Cartularium Eerste Zwartenboek, fol. 55 r-v.

17. According to notes in the *Register van de wetsvernieuwingen* a letter was published indeed: '*zekere commissie*': Bruges, municipal archives, Oud archief, 114, RW 1468-1501, fol. 172r.

18. I.L.A. Diegerick, ed., 'Correspondance des magistrats d'Ypres, députés à Gand et à Bruges, pendant les troubles de Flandre sous Maximilien, duc d'Autriche, roi des romains etc.', *Annales de la Société d'émulation pour l'étude de l'histoire et des antiquités de la Flandre*, 13 (1851-1854), pp. 3-142 at p. 64.

to send a delegation to Ghent in order to inspect the privilege and copy the text.[19] Only when the governors of Ypres were completely convinced that the text was valid, they grant Ghent the right to choose and install a new bench of aldermen in the town.

During a crisis in medieval Flanders the initiative of the ritual change of power was often changed. Every time this happened, the same problem was posed: the rebels were afraid that the legitimacy of the ritual would be questioned. The status of the deputies was crucial in this perspective: their mandate should have a strong legal basis. In 1477 a revolt broke out in Ypres. The inhabitants of the town then took the initiative to install a new bench of aldermen; however, they were obliged to ask Mary of Burgundy for an official corps of deputies delegated on her behalf.[20] According to a chronicle, the presence of these delegates was only pro forma, since they were not allowed to have an actual say in the election and composition of the town's council. They just functioned as puppets to grant the ritual legitimacy.[21] When Ghent revolted against Maximilian in November 1487, the rebels first asked the ruler to send deputies to the town.[22] Only when he refused to grant their request, did the town decide to follow an alternative scenario that was stipulated in their privileges. The latter was no option for Bruges, since the privileges of this town did not formulate such a possibility. Therefore it was necessary to follow the traditional scenario and integrate the essential phase in which the official mandate of the deputies was demonstrated. This official opening was part of the core of the ritual, since it had to legitimize the election of the municipality. When this aspect was changed, there was a risk that the whole ritual would be undermined, and its legitimacy questioned.

3.2. The oath-formulae

Every year, the newly elected aldermen and councillors of Bruges swore a solemn oath during the ritual of their installation. The ducal coun-

---

19. '*Meester Jan Coene van dat hij betaelt hadde Pietren vander Muelue, secretaris van scepenen van der kuere in Ghend, van eenen vidimisse inhoudende dat de wet ende twee dekenen van der voors. stede gheauctoriseert zijn in Vlaendren wetten ende andere officiers te vermakene 3 l. 10 s.*': Brussels, Algemeen Rijksarchief, Rk, Stadsrekeningen Ieper, 38712, fol. 99v.

20. '*par les commissaires a ce commis par la duchesse sur la requete du commun*': Brussels, Royal Library, Fonds Merghelynck, 103 II, fol. 123r.

21. I.L.A. Diegerick, ed., 'Episode de l'histoire d'Ypres sous le régne de Marie de Bourgogne 1477', *Annales de la Société d'émulation pour l'étude de l'histoire et des antiquités de la Flandre*, second series, 6 (1848), pp. 423-476 at p. 451.

22. Ghent, municipal archives, Oud archief, Stadscharters 752.

tal, representing the source of the aldermen's power, received these legally binding promises. In Bruges, this was a public event, witnessed by the inhabitants of the town. According to several sources this audience used to wait until al least seven aldermen had taken their vows and then returned home. In the municipal archives of Bruges a number of medieval oath-formulae are preserved.[23] These texts show that the aldermen swore to be loyal servants of the count and the town. They promised to pass righteous judgements and that they would protect orphans and widows. Moreover, they stated that their future conduct would not be influenced by emotions such as hate, love or envy. The councillors on their turn had to promise that they would advise wisely and keep the secret of the meetings.

In the ritual transfer of power these oaths played a crucial part. The goal this oath taking aimed at was twofold. On the one hand, these solemn promises marked the new social status of the town's governors. With these vows they were officially installed in their new function, an action which strove to legitimize their position. On the other hand the formulae summed up a great number of guidelines the new officials had to respect in the future. In doing so, the oath also had a moralizing character, since it was meant to legally bind the actions of the municipality to a certain amount of rules.[24]

The sources that describe the events on 12 February 1488 state that the formula of the aldermen's oath was adapted to the political context. According to these chronicles the aldermen no longer promised to be loyal to Maximilian, but to serve Philip the Fair and the Three Members of Flanders instead.[25] Later the same year, the representatives of the nine

23. Oath from 1432: Bruges, municipal archives, Oud archief, 114, registers van de wetsvernieuwingen 1422-1443, fol. 163 r-v; ca. 1468: Bruges, municipal archives, Oud archief, 114, registers van de wetsvernieuwingen, 1468-1501, fol. 290v; ca. 1477: Bruges, municipal archives, Oud archief, 114, registers van de wetsvernieuwingen, 1468-1501, fol. 291v.

24. About the significance of medieval oaths: J. van Leeuwen, 'Schepeneden in de Lage Landen. Een eerste verkenning van hun betekenis, overlevering en formulering (dertiende tot zestiende eeuw)', *Jaarboek voor middeleeuwse geschiedenis*, 6 (2003), pp. 112-160; Idem, 'Municipal Oaths, Political Virtues and the Centralised State. The Adaptation of Oaths of Office in Fifteenth Century Flanders', *Journal of Medieval History*, 31 (2005), 185-210. L. Kolmer, *Promissorische Eide im Mittelalter* (Kallmünz, 1989); P. Prodi, *Das Sakrament der Herrschaft. Der politische Eid in der Verfassungsgeschichte des Okzidents*, Schriften des Italienisch-Deutschen Historischen Instituts in Trient, Band 11 (Berlin, 1997).

25. *Het boeck van al 't gene datter geschiedt is binnen Brugghe sichtent jaer 1477, 14 februarii tot 1491*, C. Carton, ed., Maetschappy der Vlaemsche bibliophilen, derde serie, 2 (Ghent, 1859), pp. 183; Nicolaes Despars, *Cronijcke van den lande ende graefscepe van Vlaenderen van de jaeren 405 tot 1492*, J. De Jonghe, ed., 4 vols. (Brugge, 1837-1840), IV, pp. 343; Anthonis de Roovere, *Excellente Cronike van Vlaenderen*, ed. W. Vorsterman (Antwerp, 1531) (Antwerp, Stadsbibliotheek, KW. 7475), fol. 230ᵛ.

members of the town's population demanded that these changes should be officially promulgated. They wished that every new official in the future should swear a similar promise.[26] This reformulation was of great importance, since the clause that referred to the source of the aldermen's power was adapted to the historical context. With this significant change, Bruges openly joined the rebellious party.

Unfortunately, the actual formula used on this occasion did not survive. However, examples from other towns can illustrate how the text of the formula might have been rewritten. The oath sworn by the new municipality in Ghent on 4 November 1487 has been transcribed in a charterbook of the town. The oath of the aldermen in Ypres, taken in February 1488 has also survived. In both formulae the opening clause refers explicitly to Philip the Fair and the Members of Flanders. In Ypres its was added that the new governors should stay in office until other measures could be taken. Obviously, the resigning aldermen were careful not to damage possible future relations with Maximilian.[27] As stated earlier, these governors were not entirely convinced that the rebels were entitled to select the bench of aldermen in Ypres. In Ghent the rebels added some explicit references to peace-treaties and privileges in the benefit of the town.[28] Presumably, the latter also occurred in Bruges. In September 1488 a new municipality had to be installed. Again, the town of Ghent took the initiative for this transfer of power. Four representatives were sent to Bruges, a letter of delegation legitimated their position. In this letter, it was stated that these deputies had to take an oath from the new aldermen in Bruges. They had to take care that the formula of this oath referred to the peace-treaties of 1482 and 1488: two texts that were to the detriment of Maximilian.[29]

During other revolts the oath of the aldermen was changed as well. The rebels carefully adapted the formula to the political context in which they were used. In 1467, for example a crowd in Ghent threatened to start a revolt if the vow of the aldermen was not changed. They specifically asked that the text wouldn't refer to a much-hated treaty.[30] Moreover, the

26. O. Delepierre, ed., 'Marie de Bourgogne et Maximilien', *Annales de la Societé d'émulation pour l'histoire et les antiquités de la Flandre Occidentale*, 4 (1842), pp. 215-249 at 237.

27. J.-J. Lambin, *Geschiedkundige onderzoekingen op de aloude aenstellinge van den voogd en van de schepenen en raeden der stad Ypre* (Ypres, 1815), pp. 15-16.

28. 1485: Ghent, municipal archives, Oud archief, reeks 93, 7/G, Cartularium Eerste Zwartenboek, fol. 35r 1487: fol. 34v.

29. Bruges, municipal archives, Oud archief, 96, Cartularium Groenenboek B, fol. 69r.

30. V. Gaillard, *Archives du conseil de Flandre ou recueil de documents inédits relatifs à l'histoire politique, judiciaire, artistique et littéraire* (Ghent, 1856), pp. 171-174.

ruler could also take the initiative to rewrite the solemn promises whenever he felt the need for it. In 1485 Maximilian conquered Ghent. The
archduke then installed a new bench of aldermen and composed a new
oath-formula, referring explicitly to his triumph.[31] Such adjustments could
be so radical that the swearing of a new oath could sometimes suffice to
bind the aldermen to the political context. The formula then reflected the
altered hierarchy of power in which the aldermen had to act.

The oath-formulae belonged to the core of the ritual. Their adaptation
altered the political position of Bruges completely and thus changed the
general meaning of the action intensively. The conduct of the mayor in
Bruges shows the impact of this change very clearly. This governor first
refused to swear his oath according to the new formula. Eventually, he
obeyed, but reluctantly.[32]

3.2. The ritual space

Traditionally the ritual transfer of power in Bruges was staged in the
richly decorated town hall, located on the Burg (central square) of the
town. In this magnificent setting, the countal deputies were welcomed by
the resigning municipality and presented to the public. Moreover, the
names of the new aldermen were proclaimed from this building and these
new governors swore their oaths here. The election of the councillors and
mayors was situated in the council chamber on the first floor. The town
hall formed the symbol of the wealth, autonomy and power of Bruges.
Statues, paintings and other decorations referred to the values and norms
that a good municipality should respect both during jurisdiction and in
governing the town. Besides that, various references to the countal
dynasty were made, for example in coats of arms and portraits of
deceased counts, dukes and duchesses. These rulers were the source of
the municipality's power and with their depiction the various levels of
power in the town and county were mirrored. During the ritual the participants were presented in this framework, which at the same time wished
to legitimate their status and moralize their future conduct. The newly
elected aldermen and councillors were thus separated from the other
burghers: a visual sign that emphasized their new status.[33] Therefore, the

31. Ghent, municipal archives, Oud archief, reeks 93, 7/G, Cartularium Zwartenboeck,
fol. 35r.
32. Nicolaes Despars, *Cronijcke*, IV, pp. 327-328.
33. About Flemish townhalls: R. van Uytven, 'Flämische Belfriede und südnieder-
ländische städtische Bauwerke im Mittelalter: Symbol und Mythos', in *Information, Kommunikation und Selbstdarstellung in mittelalterlichen Gemeinden*, eds. A. Haverkamp and

town hall as setting for the yearly transfer of power offered many advantages to express the significance of this ritual for the town. It was an authoritative space that could only be used by competent persons. The town hall was no neutral space, but communicated several values and norms that were also emphasized during the ritual transfer of power, for example the importance of impartiality and rightfulness. Thus, this building did not just function as the background of the ritual; on the contrary, this meaningful setting influenced the meaning of the actions that were staged there.[34]

Several sources about the events in February 1488 indicate that the rebellious transfer of power was staged in a different location to the traditional one. The rebels organized the ritual in the town's belfry, situated on the Market Square of Bruges. The presentation of the deputies and the proclamation of the new aldermen were certainly situated there.[35] In medieval Bruges, the belfry served important political functions as the depository of the town's treasury and archives. The town bell, which formed the symbol of the town's autonomy, was situated in the tower as well. Traditionally, new regulations, verdicts and exiles were proclaimed from the balcony of this building, just like important peace-treaties and ducal ordinances. Moreover, the belfry also served military functions, since guardians were installed on the tower to watch over the town and the municipal arms and banners were stored here. In medieval Flanders these belfries were traditionally the focus of collective action; particularly during a conflict the belfry and the marketplace formed the centre of the revolt.[36] In February 1488 Bruges was in a crisis. The guilds gathered on the market and lined up under their banners. The leaders of the action communicated with them from the balcony of the Belfry. For the ritual change in power the rebels decided not to leave this location but to move the actions to the central space where the revolt was demonstrated. In

E. Müller-Luckner (München, 1998), pp. 125-159; P. Stabel, 'The Market-Place and Civic Identity in Late Medieval Flanders', in *Shaping Urban Identity in Late Medieval Europe – L'apparition d'une identité urbaine dans l'Europe du bas moyen âge*, eds. M. Boone and P. Stabel, Studies in Urban Social, Economic and Political History of the Medieval and Early Modern Low Countries, no. 11 (Leuven-Apeldoorn, 2000), pp. 43-64.

34. In medieval Ghent the townhall was also appropriated for the yearly ritual of the *Wetsvernieuwing*: J. van Leeuwen, 'Het decor van een machtswissel. Ruimtegebruik bij de Gentse wetsvernieuwing in de vijftiende eeuw', *Handelingen der maatschappij voor geschiedenis en oudheidkunde te Gent, Nieuwe Reeks*, 57 (2003), pp. 47-70.

35. Bruges, municipal archives, Oud archief, 114, Registers van de wetsvernieuwingen, 1468-1501, fol. 172r; *Het boeck van al 't gene*, pp. 183; Nicolaes Despars, *Cronijcke*, IV, pp. 343.

36. Van Uytven, 'Flämische Belfriede'; Stabel, 'The Market-Place', pp. 53-54.

doing so, the members of the guilds could witness the events, without having to break up their occupation.

The decision to move the action to the Belfry was mainly motivated by the wish to involve the rebellious burghers more intensively. They could witness and control the event, two aspects that were of major importance in medieval theories of participation. According to these conceptions the power of the town's governors had to be based on the consensus of the inhabitants. This approval could only be realized when the crowd was involved in the actions of the leading officials, at least as witnesses.[37] During revolts this participation was often expanded considerably. In a crisis crowds indeed sought to control the ritual change in power. In 1449 the guilds of Ghent assembled armed in front of the town hall when the rumour was spread that the election was not according to the rules. A similar thing happened in 1451.[38]

The historical context in February 1488 explained why the ritual transfer of power was situated in the belfry of Bruges and not as usual in the town hall. While this change was indeed significant for the ritual's meaning, the belfry also had many aspects in common with the usual setting. Both the town hall and the belfry were authoritative buildings, which could only be used by the governors of the town. They both were richly decorated and thus referred to the power and wealth of the town. Coats of arms demonstrated the various levels of power in the county in both buildings. The belfry's official status did not endanger the ritual's meaning, but strengthened the position of the newly elected governors and thus visually underlined their new status in the town.

3.4. The positions of power in the town

After 1477 the old scenario of the municipal elections was reinstated in Bruges. The ducal deputies chose the aldermen. These governors in

---

37. U. Meier, 'Konsens und Kontrolle. Der Zusammenhang von Bürgerrecht und politischer Partizipation im spätmittelalterlichen Florenz', in *Stadtregiment und Bürgerfreiheit. Handlungsspielräume in deutschen und italienischen Städten des Späten Mittelalters und der Frühen Neuzeit*, eds. K. Schreiner and U. Meier (Göttingen, 1994), pp. 147- 187; K. Schreiner, 'Teilhabe, Konsens und Autonomie. Leitbegriffe kommunaler Ordnung in der politischen Theorie des späten Mittelalters und der frühen Neuzeit', in *Theorien kommunaler Ordnung in Europa*, eds. P. Blickle and E. Müller-Luckner. Schriften des Historischen Kollegs. Kolloquien, 36 (München, 1996), pp. 35-74.

38. Jan Van de Vijvere, *Chronijcke van Ghendt*, ed. F. De Potter (Ghent, 1885) pp. 11-14; *Dagboek van Gent van 1447 tot 1470 met een vervolg van 1477 tot 1515*, ed. V. Fris, ed. (Ghent, 1901-1904), I, pp. 74-78 and 128. More details on the role of the audience in the ritual transfer of power in J. van Leeuwen, 'Ritueel en publiek. De rol van de toeschouwers bij de wetsvernieuwing in Gent, Brugge en Ieper (15de eeuw)', *Tijdschrift voor Geschiedenis*, 117 (2004), pp. 321-337.

their turn elected the councillors and the mayors of the town. Moreover, it was stipulated that the seats on the bench of aldermen were distributed among the nine official sections of the town's population.[39] Until 1485 this course was registered yearly in the *Registers van de wetsvernieuwing*[40].

On 2 February 1488 Maximilian changed some important aspects of this ritual. He issued that it was no longer obliged to select representatives of the nine sections of the town's population. Craftsmen were still allowed to participate, but it was no longer necessary to recruit them from a particular section and they were not entitled to a steady number of seats.[41] Probably, the emperor took these measures in order to favour the patricians so that they would support him in the crisis. However, only a few days later, Maximilian was imprisoned. We can assume that the rebels were not likely to obey these rules.

When the aldermen were replaced on 12 February 1488, deputies from Ghent acted as the official initiators of the ritual. According to a note in the *Register* they did not just elect the aldermen, but they also selected the councillors and the mayors. In short: it seems that the scenario from 1477 for the choice of the councillors and mayors was not implemented.[42] Probably, this was due to the rebellious context in which the ritual took place, although we do not find any traces of this scenario after 1485. We do see that eight newcomers to the municipal government were installed. This renewal of political personnel was important, although it did not mean a complete breach with the preceding regime. During other revolts

39. A.Vandewalle, 'De Brugse stadsmagistraat en de deelname van de ambachten aan het bestuur, 14de-15de eeuw', in *De Vlaamse instellingen tijdens het ancien régime: recent onderzoek in nieuw perspectief. Symposium georganiseerd te Brugge op 18 mei 1998*, eds. W. Prevenier and B. Augustijn, Miscellanea archivistica. Studia 91 (Brussels, 1999), pp. 27-40; J. Mertens, 'Brugge en Gent. De vertegenwoordiging van de "leden" in de stadsmagistraat', in *Qui valet ingenio. Liber amicorum Johan Decavele, aangeboden t.g.v. zijn 25-jarig ambtsjubileum als stadsarchivaris van Gent*, eds. J. De Zutter, L. Charles and A. Capiteyn (Ghent, 1996), pp. 385-391.
40. On this source, see: A. Vandewalle, 'Bronnen van het stadsarchief. De wetsvernieuwingen', *Archiefleven. Nieuwsbrief van het stadsarchief van Brugge*, 4 (1997), pp. 2-3.
41. Bruges, municipal archives, Oud archief, 99, Politieke oorkonden, eerste reeks, 1228. Comments: Janssens, '*Macht*', p. 11.
42. The Register does not refer to this phase of the ritual, between 1477 and 1484 this separate election of the councillors was recorded yearly. However, this formed no definite proof, since on 17 April 1482 the Register stated that the ducal deputies proclaimed the councillors, but other notes show that these governors were elected by the aldermen: Bruges, municipal archives, Oud archief, 114, Registers van de wetsvernieuwingen, 1468-1501, fol. 123v.

the majority of the bench of aldermen could consist of newcomers, but that wasn't the case in 1488.[43]

In general, it is striking that the rebels during the election of new aldermen never developed an entirely new scenario, not even in those circumstances when they had the power to do so. On the contrary, we often see that the rebels stick to the customary course of the ritual, reinstall an older scenario or appropriate traditions from a related form of symbolic communication. Does this mean that the recognizability of the ritual was of more importance than the urge to enlarge local participation in the elections? Or, does it, on the other hand, show that the ritual in fact played a minor part and that the struggle for power in the county was situated in other domains? The latter seems to have been often the case. During the revolt in Bruges in 1488 additional officials were installed, although it is not as clear how these persons were selected. On 14 February nine persons were chosen, each one representing a guild of the town's population. These men were a kind of inspectors who had to keep the nine sections informed about the decisions of the aldermen. Moreover, the inhabitants of the town were consulted about important measures. These nine representatives controlled the government in Bruges completely, since the aldermen were not allowed to take any decisions without their consent.[44] The political grievances of these sections are summarized in a long letter of complaints in which they asked for example to possess a copy of all the town's privileges.[45]

As a result of the revolt the power of the town government was diminished to the advantage of a broader group of representatives. Such a shift of power happened regularly during Flemish revolts. Although new benches of aldermen and councillors were installed, the actual government rested in the hands of other institutions or additional officials. A good example of this is the Brugean revolt of 1436. During the crisis, the great council of the town controlled political decision making. Moreover, in 1437, twenty-four wise men were chosen to support the aldermen and govern the town.[46] During uprisings in September 1490, the major part

---

43. W.P. Blockmans, 'Mutaties van het politiek personeel in de steden Gent en Brugge tijdens een periode van regimewisselingen: het laatste kwart van de 15de eeuw', in *Bronnen voor de geschiedenis van de instellingen in België – Sources de l'histoire des institutions de la Belgique. Handelingen van het Colloquium te Brussel. Actes du Colloque de Bruxelles 15-18.IV.1975*, ed. H. De Scheppers (Brussels, 1977), pp. 92-103 at 98-99.

44. Anthonis de Roovere, *Excellente cronike*, fol. 230ᵛ; Nicolaes Despars, *Cronijcke*, IV, pp. 343. Comments: Janssens, 'Macht', pp. 22-24.

45. Edited in: Delepierre, 'Marie de Bourgogne'.

46. J. Dumolyn, *De Brugse opstand van 1436-1438* (Kortrijk-Heule, 1997), pp. 265.

of the aldermen flew from the town, which was then governed by repre-sentatives of the nine sections.[47] In Ghent, we see that during various revolts the power in the town was in the hands of the great council and one or more captains representing the town's inhabitants. Both institutions diminished the power of the aldermen severely.[48]

It is remarkable that the additional officials in Bruges were installed two days after the election of new aldermen and councillors in 1488. Their selection and inauguration was not combined with the traditional ritual, but was staged separately. In doing so, their appointment did not blatantly offend against tradition. Moreover it showed that the real change in power did not happen during the customary transfer of power, but separately. Possibly, the rebels staged this in a new ritual, inspired by the traditional one. Unfortunately, no descriptions of this event survive.

4. Conclusions

This article sought to explore the elaboration of an important civic rit-ual in rebellious times. It wished to demonstrate if the ritual election and installation of the aldermen in Bruges was coloured by the rebellious con-text in 1488. How did the rites of rebellion influence the ritual transfer of power? And to what extent were changes imposed to the traditional elaboration of this solemn event?

In the first place the rebels were interested to legitimize the political status of the newly elected aldermen. In order to do so, traditional means were employed such as the staging of the event in an authoritative space. The legal foundation of the aldermen's power was expressed by publi-cizing a privilege from the French king. Thus, the rebels creatively adapted one of the basic elements of the ritual. Moreover, in the oaths sworn during the event references to fundamental changes in the politi-cal situation were integrated.

Secondly, the rebels wanted to legally bind the newly elected aldermen to their objectives. Therefore, they added some important clauses to the existing oath-formulae. The new governors had to swear these promises publicly and in doing so they guaranteed that they would live up to these expectations.

47. Anthonis de Roovere, *Excellente cronike*, fol. 270r.
48. See, M. Boone, *Gent en de Bourgondische hertogen ca. 1384 – ca. 1453 Een soci-aal-politieke studie van een staatsvormingsproces* (Brussels, 1990).

Thirdly, the rebels made sure that the crowd could witness the change in power without having to break up their occupation of the market-square. This publicity had to strengthen the relationship between the rebellious crowds and their leaders. The guilds were thus able to control the event, which formed an essential part of the medieval theory of participation. However, this participation of the town's guilds was not just symbolically enlarged. The rebels also introduced a new board of nine officials who had to control the aldermen and could thus leave a decisive mark on the town politics.

These three strategies were not exceptional. During other revolts and in other towns the same techniques were employed to adapt the ritual change in power to the objectives of the rebels. The enlarged participation and the changed initiative of the event can be labeled as traditional rebellious means. However, rulers also used the reformulation of the oath-formulae in a political crisis.

The ritual transfer of power on 12 February 1488 seems to have been conceived as a legitimate ritual. The validity of the actions was not questioned, since the rebels did follow the traditional scenario of the event. However, they took a major risk. It is indeed striking that the margins of the event such as banquets and bell ringing, were not changed at all. On the contrary, the rebels adapted the core of the event: the demonstration of the legal source of the aldermen's power and the oath-formulae. In doing so, they tried to approach the traditional scenario as closely as possible. Thus the traditions and the rites of rebellion were carefully balanced. That the rebels wished to enhance the recognizability of the ritual is also shown by the events on 14 February. Two days after the ritual nine additional officials were appointed. Their election and installation was not combined with the transfer of power, since this addition might damage the recognizability of the ritual and thus might have endangered its legitimacy. Eventually, this additional appointment undermined the meaning of the ritual transfer in power. The real change in power in the town was not situated in the ritual election of new aldermen and councillors, but in the installation of nine representatives of the town's population.

Katholieke Universiteit Leuven

Mario DAMEN

GIVING BY POURING:
THE FUNCTION OF GIFTS OF WINE IN THE CITY OF LEIDEN
(14TH-16TH CENTURIES)

Introduction

In 1520-1521 Albert Dürer made a journey through the Netherlands. In a note-book he registered accurately his encounters and the presents he exchanged. In Antwerp, for example, he dined sumptuously with some painters and their wives. After dinner, a messenger from the city council arrived and he handed over four jugs of wine to Dürer saying that it was a gift in honour of the guest to show the city's good intentions. Dürer thanked the messenger and offered him his services.[1] The wine did not only function as a token of honour but also to put the visitor in the right mood, as he would eventually do something in return in the future. So there was an expectation of reciprocity, which implied an exchange of material goods or services.

City administrations all over Europe used to offer gifts of wine to dignitaries and authorities who visited the city. This act of courtesy and hospitality had become a custom since the thirteenth century, although it can be traced even further back; the so-called *libatio*, the communal ritual drinking, was a binding factor for social relationships in Merovingian and Carolingian times. In the late Middle Ages the custom became institutionalised in the cities.[2] Wine gifts were a token of respect for a visitor and served as a sign of recognition of the services the visitor had rendered in the past or would render in the future to the benefit of the city. Therefore, wine gifts can be viewed as a form of generalised reciprocity: the countergift is not specified and it is not clear that or when it is going to come.[3]

---

1. *Albert Dürers dagverhaal zijner Nederlandsche reize in de jaren 1520 en 1521, met belangrijke aanteekeningen opgehelderd* (The Hague, 1840), pp. 25-26.

2. Jan Dhondt, *Das frühe mittelalter* (Frankfurt am Main, 1968), pp. 118-120. Alain Derville, 'Les pots-de-vin dans le dernier tiers du XVe siècle (d'après les comptes de Lille et de Saint-Omer)', in *1477. Het algemene en de gewestelijke privilegiën van Maria van Bourgondië voor de Nederlanden*, ed. W.P. Blockmans (Kortrijk-Heule, 1985), p. 451.

3. Marshall Sahlins, 'On the sociology of primitive exchange', in *The gift: an interdisciplinary perspective* ed. Aafke Komter (Amsterdam, 1996), pp. 34-35.

In this contribution an attempt is made to demonstrate on the one hand how the city administration of Leiden used the wine gift in its contacts with the world outside the city walls, and on the other hand what function wine had during political and religious ceremonies within the city. Leiden was the third of the six so-called capital or major cities of the county of Holland. Around 1500 the city counted approximately 12,000 inhabitants. The economy depended largely on the production of beer and cloth, goods that had a good market abroad.[4] Together with Haarlem, Leiden is one of the best-documented cities of Holland. The sources used for this paper are mainly the accounts of the burgomasters and treasurers and in addition the resolution books of the local council, the *vroedschap*. The eldest account book available, that of 1391/92, was the starting point and with intervals of twenty years the accounts until 1572/73 were studied, depending on their availability. As the investigated period covered a 160 years, changes in the use and the function of wine gifts could be detected.

In the accounts we find liquid consumption in two chapters. The costs of the wine poured in the so-called 'stedecannen', jugs, were clustered in a special chapter in the accounts. Whereas originally this chapter was titled 'Van gesceyncten wijn', that is 'poured wine', in the course of the fifteenth century it was abbreviated to 'Scheyncken'. In middledutch as in modern Dutch this means both the presentation of a gift and pouring out a liquid.[5] In addition to the chapter of 'Scheynken', another chapter called 'Cost opten huyse' existed which accounted for the meals and wine consumed by the city administration and their guests in the city hall or in a tavern elsewhere in the city. Whereas the wine gifts in the chapter 'Scheynken' were primarily destined for guests and visitors, the consumption goods registered in 'Cost opten huyse' were used by the city administration together with the guests in the city hall. There is no evidence that in Leiden a special officer was in charge of the distribution of the wine and other presents as was the case in Ghent.[6] Nevertheless, the administrative classification shows that the wine gift had become an inextricable part of city politics.

4. A recent overview is offered by *Leiden. Een geschiedenis van een Hollandse stad I. Leiden tot 1574*, ed. J.W. Marsilje (Leiden, 2002).

5. As it is in German, see Jürgen Hannig, '*Ars donandi*. Zur Ökonomie des Schenkens im frühen Mittelalter', *Geschichte in Wissenschaft und Unterricht*, 37 (1986), p. 150, and Valentin Groebner, *Liquid assets, dangerous gifts. Presents and politics at the end of the Middle Ages* (Philadelphia, 2002), p. 22.

6. Marc Boone, 'Dons et pots-de-vin, aspects de la sociabilité urbaine au bas Moyen Age. Le cas gantois pendant la période bourguignonne', *Revue du Nord*, 70 (1988), p. 473.

In his book on presents and politics in the cities of the Upper Rhine, Valentin Groebner states that the primary role of the gifts of wine was economic, because the excise tax on wine 'was the most important source of income for the municipal treasury'.[7] In other words: when pouring wine, the city administration financed its own budget. However, in Leiden this was not the case. Here the excise tax on beer was much more important than that one wine. Moreover, the wine sellers could deduct the costs of the wine poured on special occasions from the excises to be paid.[8]

A gift culture

In the major cities of Flanders, Artois and Brabant a genuine gift culture existed, as was already demonstrated by Marc Boone, Alain Derville and Raymond van Uytven.[9] They discovered a broad range of gifts, from jugs of wine to valuable silver ware and from small New Years gifts to considerable amounts of money. In the accounts of Leiden similar gifts as in Ghent, Lille, St. Omer and Louvain are found. Most of these gifts were labelled as 'hoofsheden' or courtesies. What meaning did this word have in an urban environment?

The middledutch word 'huesheit' or 'hovescheid' appears already in the second half of the thirteenth century, both in literary and administrative sources. According to the literary historian W.P. Gerritsen the word has the same meaning in both sources: a lubricant for human relationships. That lubricant could be a tip, a present, or a gratification to establish, maintain or restore the relationship between giver and receiver. On the other hand, 'hoofsheid' in general indicated a rule of conduct, not restricted to noble and princely households, which aimed to stimulate one's self control and to spare the other's sensitivity. In other words, courtly behaviour smoothed social traffic.[10] All courtesies, and among them wine, were

7. Groebner, *Liquid assets*, p. 23.

8. See on this Leiden Gemeentearchief, Secretarie-archief I (hereafter SA), 563 fol. 118r.

9. Boone, 'Dons et pots-de-vin'; A. Derville, 'Pots-de-vin, cadeaux, rackets, patronage. Essai sur les mécanismes de décisions dans l'État bourguignon', *Revue du Nord,* 56 (1976), pp. 341-364; R. van Uytven, 'Vers un autre colloque: hiérarchies sociales et prestige au moyen age et aux temps modernes', in *Sociale structuren en topografie van armoede en rijkdom in de 14e en 15e eeuw. Methodologsche aspecten en resultaten van recent onderzoek*, eds. W. Prevenier, R. van Uytven and E. van Cauwenberghe (Ghent, 1986), pp. 160, 174-175.

10. Norbert Elias, *Het civilisatieproces: sociogenetische en psychogenetische onderzoekingen* (Utrecht, 1982), p. 91; W.P. Gerritsen, 'Wat is hoofsheid? Contouren van een middeleeuws cultuurverschijnsel', in *Hoofse cultuur. Studies over een aspect van de middeleeuwse cultuur,* eds. R.E.V. Stuip en C. Vellekoop, (Utrecht, 1983), pp. 26-30, 39-40.

offered 'in eerbairheit van der stede' that is, to maintain or, even better, to increase the honour or reputation of the city. Thus contemporaries did realise that both solid and liquid gifts could play an important role in the maintenance of the social and political network of the city.

Wine was the pre-eminent lubricant of the late Middle Ages. As pure water was lacking, wine was consumed on a far larger scale than nowadays. Wine had (and still has) a higher status than beer and that is why it was the most adequate liquid to use within social and political relationships. This becomes very clear in 1512. On March 1 of that year, stormy weather provoked the collapse of the tower of the church of St. Peter, which functioned as archive of the town administration. As a result the documents were buried under the debris of the tower that was scattered all over. A group of fullers, who were ordered to carry away the debris, found the privileges of the town and took them to the house of the bailiff where at that time the bench of aldermen was deliberating. The aldermen awarded themselves some 22 litres of wine, whereas the fullers received two barrels of beer as a reward.[11]

The wine was presented to guests in tin jugs with a content of 4,85 litre. On the lid of the jug the coat of arms of the city, the keys of St. Peter, was engraved so that it was clear who was the donor of the wine and the owner of the jug. The wine was not taken home but consumed directly by the receiver and his retinue. The jug was given back so that it could be used again. The wine most often given, white Rhine wine, was the most popular wine in the Northern Netherlands. The less expensive red wine was poured only occasionally.[12] Until 1500 the more expensive sweet wines from the Mediterranean, such as malvoisie and romani, were given especially to high-ranked visitors (for example the count, a papal legate) or on special occasions (for example the auditing of an account, the election of the burgomasters).

A quantitative approach

In order to quantify the gift-giving policy of the city-administration, a number of figures were collected from the accounts for the period 1392-

11. SA 592 fol. 68r. On the collapse of the tower of St. Peter: J.C. Overvoorde en J.W. Verburgt, *Archief der secretarie van de stad Leiden 1253-1575* (Leiden, 1937) pp. xxii-xxiii and Frans van Mieris, *Beschryving der stad Leyden* I (Leiden, 1762), p. 26. I thank drs. Ed van der Vlist for these references.

12. A. Meerkamp van Embden, *Stadsrekeningen van Leiden, 1390-1434* I (Amsterdam, 1913) (hereafter ME I), p. 240: the treasurer of Holland receives two jugs of red wine; in July 1452 the president of the Council of Flanders gets red wine SA 523, fol. 81r); deputies from Gouda receive red wine in December 1492 (SA 563, fol. 82v).

1573. Of course these figures are only indicative since I took a (select) sample of no more than ten. Nevertheless, some trends become clear. Table 1 shows the total amount of money spent on wine and meals in absolute figures and as a percentage of the total expenses of the city. In 1434 most money was spent on wine and meals, namely 424 pounds Hollands. In that year a master mason had to work 1272 days to earn this amount of money. Nevertheless, the costs represented less than two per cent of the total expenses of the city in that year. In contrast, in 1392 less money was spent, but the costs for wine and meals took ten per cent of the total expenses. Still, it is evident that the city administration did relatively spend not much money on wine and meals; in most of the years less than one per cent. Furthermore, in the course of time the amount of money spent on this purpose decreased both in absolute and relative figures

Table 1. Costs of wine and meals (pounds of 30 groats[13])			
Year	Total expenditure	Costs of wine and meals	Percentage
1392	1,727	172	10
1413	13,068	355	2.7
1434	25,117	424	1.7
1452	24,534	328	1.3
1473	41,726	266	0.64
1493	25,514	255	1
1513	55,690	131	0.23
1533	40,229	74	0.18
1556	31,591	264	0.84
1573	37,671	35	0.09

The figures of Table 2 confirm this decrease. For this table I counted the number of visitors who received jugs of wine, a meal or wine in another form than in jugs. First, the number of visitors increased steadily, up to 151 in 1434. After 1473, however, a sharp decline set in with ten visitors in 1573 as an absolute low. Of course political circumstances have influenced these figures. In 1434, for example, a

13. For the years 1555/56 and 1572/73 the amounts of money in the account are pounds of 40 groats and therefore converted into pounds of 30 groats.

constant flow of councillors from The Hague came to Leiden to restore law and order after a riot had broken out. Conversely, hardly any guests visited the city in 1572, a year of much political tension when of Leiden had chosen the side of William of Orange. In the Bavarian and Burgundian period, which is until 1477, the city offered wine and meals to visitors on average one to three times a week, whereas afterwards in the Habsburg period this frequency was only one to three times a month.

How to explain this decrease? One is tempted to say that the visitors still came but that they were not offered as much as in the preceding period. Leiden suffered big financial problems from the last decade of the 15th century onwards, due to increasing tax demands from the central government and the burden of life annuities sold in the past. However, as was shown the costs of wine and meals represented only a small percentage of total expenses of the city. Another explanation could be that political decisions in the Habsburg period were increasingly made at a central level, in meetings with the representatives of the prince in The Hague or Brussels for example. The same kind of centralisation can be observed at another level. Whereas in the Bavarian and Burgundian period meetings of the representatives of the towns and nobles often took place in Leiden, in the Habsburg period they preferred The Hague as a central meeting place.[14] As I will demonstrate the officers of the prince and the city deputies were two of the most important groups of beneficiaries of wine gifts, so a decrease in the frequency of visits of these men will be noted strongly in the total number of visitors. However, similar research for Haarlem showed that winegifts for representatives of the towns did not diminish in the sixteenth century, so in that town bilateral consultations remained important.[15]

---

14. In the period 1477-1494 averagely three times a year a meeting of the estates was held in Leiden, whereas in the period 1506-1515 the frequency was only once a year. H. Kokken, *Steden en Staten. Dagvaarten van steden en Staten van Holland onder Maria van Bourgondië en het eerste regentschap van Maximiliaan van Oostenrijk (1477-1494)* (The Hague, 1991), p. 131 and J.P. Ward, *The cities and states of Holland (1506-1515). A participative system of government under strain* (unpublished dissertation; Leiden, 2001), p. 87.

15. Arie van Steensel, 'Giften aan vrienden en invloedrijken. Schenkgewoonten van de stad Haarlem tijdens de Bourgondische en Habsburgse tijd', *Holland*, 37 (2005), pp. 1-22.

Table 2. Wine and meals given to visitors in Leiden (1392-1573)										
Number of jugs	1	2	3	4	5	6	7	8	Total	Wine (not in jugs) and meals	General totals
1392	2	47	-	11	-	-	-	-	60	15	75
1413	-	39	1	16	-	-	-	8	64	26	90
1434	4	22	-	11	1	2	1	-	41	110	151
1452	-	17	1	10	-	1	-	-	29	25	54
1473	-	38	-	24	-	1	-	-	63	10	73
1493	-	17	-	9	-	1	-	-	27	13	40
1513	-	4	-	10	-	-	-	1	15	7	22
1533	-	8	-	8	-	1	-	-	17	3	20
1556	-	16	-	15	-	-	-	2	33	2	35
1573	-	5	-		-	-	-	2	7	3	10
Totals	6	213	2	114	1	6	1	13	356	196	552

Table 2 shows that eight jugs (approximately 38.8 litres) was the maximum quantity of wine given. However, only thirteen dignitaries received this number of jugs, about 4 percent of totally 356 wine gifts. Most frequently, two jugs of wine (9.7 litres) were given: 213 times of the 356 wine gifts, which is about 60 percent. The second most popular gift was four jugs, given a 114 times (32 percent). The conclusion is that the standard gift was two or four jugs and only occasionally other amounts were given. The number of jugs depended of one's place in the social hierarchy as perceived by the city administration. The higher up the position on the social ladder, the more men and servants there were in the retinue of the visitor, the more jugs were needed to satisfy everybody's needs.

Beneficiaries: the prince and his servants

Who were the beneficiaries of all the gifts of wine and meals and did the city administration have a special intention distributing these gifts in kind? In Chart 1, based on data for the entire period, seven categories are distinguished: the prince, the courtiers and officers of the prince, the viscount of Leiden (the lord of Wassenaar and his family), other nobles, clergymen, city deputies and others who do not fit in these categories, mainly heemraden or dyke reeves of Rijnland, the administrative region in which Leiden was situated, foreign merchants and artists.

The count of Holland, the uppermost dignitary in the social and functional hierarchy, always received the biggest quantity of wine. Gifts of wine to the prince can be traced back to 1266 when in the first charter granted to the city Floris V stipulated that the count should receive a barrel of wine on the occasion of the confirmation of its privileges.[16] However, in the course of time the distance between the prince and the citizens was widened by the integration of Holland and Zeeland into bigger personal unions. This distance is reflected in the wine gifts. In the years under investigation, William VI of Bavaria received wine on no fewer than seven occasions in the year 1413, whereas Charles the Bold in 1473 received wine once only (on 5 February). William VI, who resided in the county during 20-50 percent of his time, was physically present and accessible for his citizens. Charles the Bold resided mainly in the southern principalities of the Netherlands and visited the county of Holland only twice, in 1468 for his inauguration and in 1473.[17] When they visited a city, they had always a specific reason; both princes came to ask the city for a contribution in the subsidies, the so-called 'beden', which were of growing importance to the income of the prince. Whereas William VI normally received eight jugs of wine, Charles the Bold received a whole barrel, the equivalent of 56 jugs or 271.6 litres of wine.[18] Is this simply an inflation of the gift to the prince or was the barrel reminiscence of the privilege of 1266? The first explanation is rather more likely: although in the Bavarian period the number of eight jugs was reserved for the count, in the Burgundian period this amount of wine was granted too to his substitute in Holland, the stadhouder or lieutenant. In the Habsburg period eight jugs were even given to high nobles.

Of course, the prince could never consume this quantity of liquid by himself and his retinue probably drank the majority of the wine. However, in addition to the barrel for Charles the Bold in 1473, fifteen high-ranking courtiers received jugs of wine. The city distinguished among these courtiers between councillors with a university degree, local officers and young nobles, who received two jugs, and prominent officers like the steward Guillaume de Bische, high nobles like the lords of Brederode,

16. Marsilje, *Leiden*, p. 59; Smit, *Vorst en onderdaan*, p. 334; *Oorkondenboek van Holland en Zeeland tot 1299. Deel: III: 1256 tot 1278*, ed. J.G. Kruisheer (Assen, 1992), p. 468 article 20.
17. Smit, *Vorst en onderdaan*, pp. 31-32, 212-219.
18. ME I, pp. 239-243; SA 549, fol. 71r.

Montfoort and Nassau, who received four jugs. The duke's substitute in Holland, stadhouder Louis of Gruuthuse, received six jugs.[19]

During the visit of the duke, the city administration invited Gruuthuse to return the next day for a joint dinner since the stadhouder had been absent from the county for such a long time, as the accounts specifically note. It is likely that the city wanted to discuss some issues with the stadhouder and there had not been enough time for this during the visit of the duke. Gruuthuse accepted the invitation and accompanied by his son Jan and the lord of Kruibeke he came to the city on 6 February 1473. They had a meal with the most prominent men from the city administration and council. This meal costed almost 12 pounds Hollands, half of the costs of the barrel of wine for the duke, but still an amount of money for which a master carpenter had to work 35 days.[20] However, the benefits at least equalled the costs. The city wanted to establish a durable relationship with important courtiers and officers like Gruuthuse. The city had consented to pay new subsidies to the duke, and now it had to be decided how much each city and community had to contribute. The stadhouder coordinated the negotiations about this so-called apportionment. Although there was a more or less fixed distributive code among the main cities, each wanted to pay as little as possible. Therefore it was important that the stadhouder was favourably disposed towards the city.

Thus, the city clearly invested to strengthen relationships with high officers like the stadhouder and other courtiers, councillors, maitres des comptes and secretaries both from the regional institutions in The Hague and the supra-regional institutions of the Burgundian and Habsburg princes. Chart 1 shows that this group consisted of 39 per cent of the beneficiaries and thus benefited most from wine and meals presented by the city. These were not only generally intended to put them in the right mood but sometimes could form a stimulus to render specific services. In September 1513, for example, the city-administration invited treasurer-general Roland le Fevre three times for dinner. These meals were more expensive than the money gift (32 pounds Hollands) he received the same month. Le Fevre was fully aware of the principle of reciprocity. His countergift consisted of a promise to do his best in order that the city could keep its privilege to choose its own mag-

19. SA 549, fols. 71r-72r.
20. SA 549, cost.

istrates. However, the services of the highest financial officer in the Habsburg state-apparatus entailed more than a promise. Later that month he helped the secretary of the city to sell 'renten' or annuities in his hometown Antwerp and in Mechelen. By selling annuities, the city borrowed money at interest to finance the subsidies it had to pay to the prince.[21] Certainly, the treasurer general would not encounter many difficulties to interest members of his extensive financial network in these high-interest-loans.

Leiden did not only pay attention to high officials but also to the local officials with whom the city had to deal on a more day-to-day basis. In the Bavarian period the baljuw or sheriff of Rijnland, the officer for judicial affairs in the area around Leiden, and the rentmeester or receiver of Noordholland, responsible for the princely domains around Leiden, received each two jugs of wine when they were newly appointed.[22] But the offerings could go beyond these courtesies. In 1433/34 the burgomasters bestowed the sheriff of Rijnland three times with wine (in total 29 mengel, that is a bit more than 35 litres) in order to be 'voirderlic', helpful, to some burghers of the town.[23] Similarly, the city approached the third local officer, the houtvester or ranger of the princely forestry next to Leiden, the Haarlemmerhout. He received special attentions when he came to the town in November 1433 to investigate damage in the forestry caused by burghers of Leiden. The burgomasters paid his expenses and meals in several inns (8 pounds Hollands) in order that he would not investigate too thoroughly: 'omdat [hij] 't scarpste op hem niet soeken en soude'.[24]

In particular the decision makers and information brokers within the state apparatus were bestowed with wine; they were the essential targets for the city administration. The lower categories of officers (clerks, doorkeepers, messengers) were bestowed in other ways: with small amounts of money ('drinking money') or with New Year's gifts.[25]

---

21. SA 592, fols. 42r, 50r-v.

22. ME I, pp. 20-21.

23. A. Meerkamp van Embden, *Stadsrekeningen van Leiden, 1390-1434*, II (Amsterdam 1914) (hereafter ME II), p. 318.

24. ME II, p. 312.

25. Mario Damen, 'Corrupt of hoofs gedrag? Geschenken en het politieke netwerk van een laat-middeleeuwse Hollandse stad', *Tijdschrift voor sociale en economische geschiedenis*, 2 (2005), pp. 68-95. See also Groebner, *Liquid assets*, pp. 142-143.

Chart 1: Beneficiaries of wine and meals in
Leiden (1392-1573)

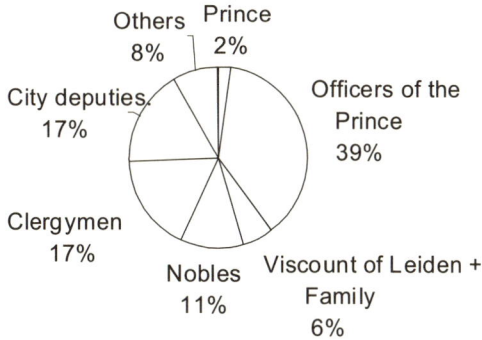

Others Prince
8%   2%

City deputies
17%

Officers of the
Prince
39%

Clergymen
17%

Nobles
11%

Viscount of Leiden +
Family
6%

Nobles and clergymen

In Chart 1 the nobles constitute a special category. Although most categories are distinguished by functional criteria, this one is based on a social criterion. In reality the percentage of 17 per cent of noble beneficiaries is an underestimate as there were clergymen and courtiers and officers of the prince who were of noble origin. So the noblemen included in this category did not occupy a function in the secular and religious hierarchies. Moreover, the gifts to the viscount of Leiden and his family (6 per cent of the gifts) were put aside.

In 1340 the lord of Wassenaar became viscount of Leiden. Until 1420 the viscount had a special relationship with the city because he had the right to appoint the schout or bailiff of the city, and the eight aldermen, who were renewed yearly. So he strongly influenced the day-to-day administration of the city.[26] Not surprisingly the viscount was a frequent visitor of the city hall. In 1391/92, for example, viscount Philip of

26. M.J. van Gent en A. Janse, 'Van ridders tot baronnen. De Wassenaers in de Middeleeuwen (1200-1523)', in *Heren van stand. Van Wassenaar 1200-2000. Achthonderd jaar Nederlandse adelsgeschiedenis*, ed. H.M. Brokken (Zoetermeer, 2000), pp. 14-16.

Wassenaar and his closest family members received wine on seven occasions.[27] In February 1413, the son of the viscount was released from captivity. At the viscount's request, the city had helped to pay the ransom. Father and son visited the city hall to celebrate his liberation and they received twice eight jugs, exceptional because they normally got only two or four jugs.[28] The city administration considered it important to stay on good terms with the viscount since those who offered him wine had generally been appointed by him before. In other words: the clients wanted to strengthen their relationship with their patron. Moreover, the viscount was one of the most influential nobles at the court of the Bavarian dukes so he could look after the interests of the city at the highest political level.

Among the other nobles who received wine we encounter members of the most important noble lineages in Holland: Van Assendelft, Van Arkel, Van Brederode, Van Egmond, and Van Montfoort. Of the nobility of Zeeland we only encounter those who were active in the household or council of the prince. The number of jugs given to these nobles increased over time. In the Bavarian and Burgundian periods they received two or four jugs, whereas in the Habsburg period most nobles received four jugs. In 1573 some nobles even received eight jugs.[29] This can be explained by the rise of the status of these noblemen who acquired domains all over the Netherlands and behaved like princes with their own court and corresponding culture.[30] Finally, only among the nobles female beneficiaries can be found. They received normally two or four jugs of wine, when they visited the city, apparently on their own; when they accompanied their husbands no special gifts of wine are mentioned.[31] Again, the city showed a courtly behaviour towards high-ranked visitors. The urban elite was concerned for its reputation and honour and probably had to make even more efforts than nobles to demonstrate this.[32]

The same is true for the wine-gifts to the clergymen. The city perceived a clearly defined hierarchy within the clergy. To give some examples: the minister of the Franciscans received two jugs, the abbess of the

27. ME I, pp. 22, 25, 26.
28. ME I, p. 238.
29. SA 643, fols. 40v-41r.
30. Hans Cools, *Mannen met macht. Edellieden en de moderne staat in de Bourgondisch-Habsburgse landen (1475-1530)* (Zutphen, 2001).
31. Winegifts to women in: ME I, pp. 24, 32, 237, 239, 240; ME II, pp. 371, 374, 375.
32. Felicity Heal, *Hospitality in early modern England* (Oxford, 1990), p. 302.

convent of Rijnsburg, close to Leiden, four jugs and the bishop of Utrecht eight jugs.[33] The hierarchy within the clergy was apparently better defined than in the court and state apparatus. The city administration maintained a special relationship with the convent of the Franciscans, founded in 1445 just outside Leiden's city walls. The friars were not only helped financially with the restoration of their buildings but were also given two, later four, jugs of wine yearly on the occasion of the most important feasts of the liturgical calendar like Christmas, Easter and Whitsuntide. Moreover, from 1465 onwards the Franciscans could collect the wine needed for the Masses free of charge.[34] In 1473, for example, no less than 209 mengel (approximately 225 litres) of malvoisie were poured for this reason.[35] The costs of this free wine increased so heavily that in 1475 the city administration decided to pay a fixed amount of money of 16 pounds Hollands to the friars instead.[36] In 1499 this amount was raised to 24 pounds as a compensation for the abolition of wine gifts on Christian holy days. Wine gifts to the Franciscans were restricted to the occasions when high functionaries of the order visited the town.[37]

Not surprisingly, the gifts of the city-administration were reciprocated. The friars invited the city governors for a meal on the day of St. Francis, October 4, or in the weeks afterwards, which, however, was paid by the city administration. This custom was continued until the 1560s.[38] The countergift of the friars went nonetheless further than this invitation. The Franciscans were essential for the religious life in most of the towns of the Netherlands because they regularly delivered sermons in several places in town. Moreover, they had a special relationship with the civil militias, they celebrated mass on the occasion of the renewal of the city-administration and had an important role in the procession of Corpus Christi.[39] An exchange took place of material goods for services, which were partly connected with the legitimacy of the political elite of the town.

---

33. SA 629, fols. 32r-33v.
34. Cunibertus Sloots, *De Minderbroeders te Leiden: ter dankbare herdenking van hun 500 jarig verblijf in deze stad* (Rotterdam, 1947), pp. 46-54.
35. SA 549, fol. 75r.
36. SA 550, fol. 83v and Sloots, *De Minderbroeders*, p. 46.
37. SA 382, fol. 519r, 616, fol. 35r and 629, fol. 32v
38. SA 616, fol. 36v.
39. Bart Ramakers, *Spelen en figuren. Toneelkunst en processiecultuur in Oudenaarde tussen middeleeuwen en moderne tijd* (Amsterdam,1996), p. 58.

City deputies

The deputies of other cities, mainly in Holland, received 17 per cent of the total amount of wine and dinners offered. City deputies regularly visited Leiden for bilateral deliberation. For example, in August 1392 two jugs of wine were given to deputies of Gouda because there was a legal dispute between the sheriff of Gouda and a burgher of Leiden.[40] Delegates visited the city also for a multilateral meeting or diet of the Estates of Holland in which the representatives of the cities and some nobles and clergymen gathered to discuss about matters concerning the whole county. In 1473 for example, the deputies of Haarlem and Amsterdam each received two jugs when they discussed the payment of the new subsidies granted to the prince.[41] Thus the wine had a clear function: it was used to confirm the settlement of a dispute or to drink to cooperation in political or financial matters.

Not only with nobles and non-nobles one stood on rank. When delegates of several cities received wine at the same time, for example during a diet, the order in which they were registered in the account reflected the order in which they had received their first charter: Dordrecht first, followed by Haarlem, Delft, Gouda and Amsterdam.[42] Except for Dordrecht[43] deputies from these cities were the most frequent visitors. Some significant differences become clear in comparison with other beneficiaries of winegifts. First, the city deputies received wine as an anonymous group and not as individuals. In the accounts they are registered as 'the city of Haarlem', 'the city-administration of Gouda' or 'the deputies of Amsterdam' and the names of the visitors are only rarely mentioned. Furthermore, throughout the investigated period the city deputies received the same amount of two jugs; no inflation of the winegift occurred. Finally, the wine gifts to city-deputies were the only ones that were given to people who were positioned on the same step of the social ladder; the deputies of Leiden would receive the same quantity of wine when they visited another city.

Wine for the urban elite

The city administration did not only pour out wine for visitors with a certain rank or prestige but was also generous to its own members and servants. On several fixed moments during the year the city poured out

40. ME I, p. 26
41. SA 549, fol. 74r.
42. See for example SA 523, fols. 77r, 81v.
43. Deputies from Dordrecht visited Leiden only three times in the investigated years: ME II, pp. 351, 374; SA 563, fol. 84v.

wine to its own benefit. The most important occasions were the election of the four burgomasters on St. Martin's eve and the celebration of Corpus Christi, the second Thursday after Whitsuntide. During these festivities a great number of people – up to 537 people with Corpus Christi in 1556[44] (see Chart 2) – were given a mengel (1.2125 litre) of wine. Among the beneficiaries were: the political elite (the members of the vroedschap or council, the bailiff, the aldermen and the burgomasters); a second group of urban officers (the clerk, the secretary, the messengers, the trumpet player and the three pipers and other subordinate servants) and a third group of others appointed by the city (for example the schoolmasters and the physicians). However, numerically the most important group were the members of the shooting fraternities, both archers and crossbowmen.

Chart 2 suggests that the number of people who received wine on St. Martin's eve increased significantly in the fifteenth century. However, in the sixteenth century the gifts of wine on the occasion of the election of the burgomasters stopped. Instead, fixed amounts of presence money were given with which one had to buy one's own wine in one of Leiden's taverns. Still, on Corpus Christi the tradition of the distribution of wine was preserved; in the course of 160 years the number of receivers of wine gifts on this occasion even tripled.

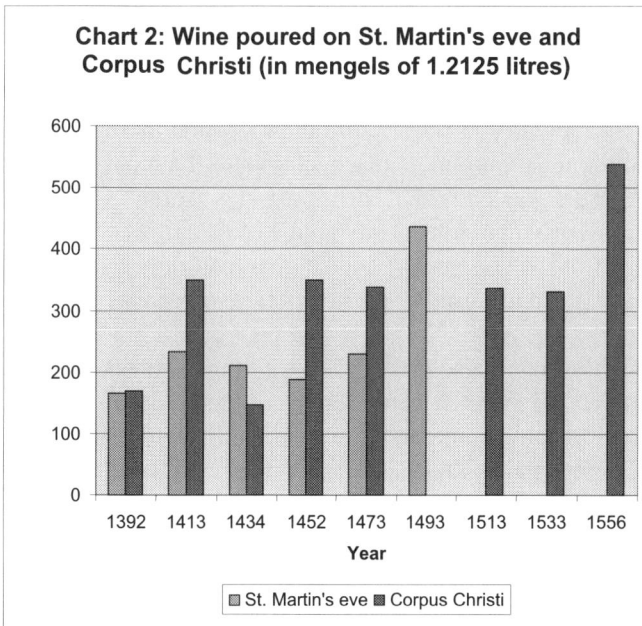

Chart 2: Wine poured on St. Martin's eve and Corpus Christi (in mengels of 1.2125 litres)

44. SA 629, fol. 35v.

Calculations for 1473 give an impression of the quantity of wine that was poured on these days. On St. Martin's eve and Corpus Christi altogether 568 people received a mengel, which implies that almost 690 litres of wine was poured.[45] During this year the city donated to visitors 178 jugs of wine, together with a barrel for the duke and 209 mengel for the Franciscans, in total almost 1390 litres of wine. This means that on the two festival days alone, the city's political elite consumed half of the quantity wine that was given to the visitors during the whole year.

Thus, the political elite of the city participated intensely in the public festivities on these two festival days. Several functions can be attributed to the distribution of wine on these days. First, with the slogan 'wine for free', the city-administration could count on a massive attendance of the political and religious ceremonies. In this way the entire political and official elite of the city became involved with the festivities which could stimulate the internal cohesion. Because of the yearly regularity of the gifts the relationship of the city with its servants was continuously renewed and confirmed. However, the range of the gifts went beyond the walls of the city hall. Both festivities were to some extent designed to legitimise the political order of the city. On St. Martin's eve both the old and the new elected burgomasters were bestowed with wine. In this way, the transfer of authority was communicated to a larger audience, although that audience was more or less limited to the political elite.[46] On Corpus Christi, however, a larger audience was reached because all those who received wine had participated in a procession through the city in which the holy sacrament was carried. In the procession the magistrate of the town had the most prominent place, closest to the monstrance in which the sacred host was carried. That is why this Corpus Christi has been interpreted as a symbol of the body politic of the city of which everybody formed part but which was of course governed only by a select few.[47] Once again the legitimisation of the political order was celebrated with wine.

This legitimisation also makes clear why the members of the shooting confraternities played such a crucial role during these festivities. The city-administration could summon these urban militias to restore order or to defend the city against attackers. As the militias should defend the city,

45. SA 549, fols. 75v, 76r-v.

46. Heal, *Hospitality in early modern England*, pp. 324-326; Groebner, *Liquid assets*, pp. 23-24.

47. Ramakers, *Spelen en figuren*, pp. 10, 59, 67. M. Carasso-Kok ed., *Geschiedenis van Amsterdam tot 1578. Een stad uit het niets* (Amsterdam, 2004), p. 431.

and with it the political elite, it was important to maintain a good relationship with them. The regular gifts of wine were a sign of this relationship, besides the fact that it was a reward for the assistance of the archers and crossbowmen during the ceremonies. Wine could even have functioned as bait for participation in the procession. As a sixteenth century chronicler from Amsterdam reports the militia-men were poured wine during the procession 'and their bellies were full before the procession had ended; such was their devotion'.[48]

In addition to these yearly wine gifts, the city contributed financially to the confraternities to cover the expenses of the special clothes the members wore, and of the shooting contests the confraternity organised.[49] The most important one was the popinjay shooting, in which the prince and/or his representatives participated regularly. In 1413 for example, when William VI participated in this contest, the costs were so high that the city-administration donated 40 pounds Hollands.[50] In 1473 stadhouder Lodewijk van Gruuthuse would participate in the popinjay shooting. The city had already financed an expensive militiaman's cape but in the end Gruuthuse had left for Flanders. Instead his two sons and some members of the Council of Holland and Zeeland were invited; it did not matter who was coming as long as the prince was represented. After the contest the dignitaries were treated generously with a big meal, financed by the city-administration.[51] During this kind of meeting the political elites of both Leiden and the Burgundian lands could establish contacts in an informal way. In years when the costs of the new subsidies had to be apportioned this could be advantageous.

Conclusion

The city administration of Leiden used the wine gift to establish and maintain its external and internal relationships. Especially in the fifteenth century, more people received more wine which caused an increase of the costs of this kind of public relations. However, during the Habsburg

48. Carasso-Kok, *Geschiedenis*, p. 420 ('dien wert op veel plaetsen de wijn ghesconcken (…) ende het buycksken wert altemet vol al eer de processie gedaen is: dit is haere devotie die sy hebben').
49. M. Carasso-Kok, '*Der stede scut*. De schutterijen in de Hollandse steden tot het einde der zestiende eeuw', in *Schutters in Holland. Kracht en zenuwen van de stad*, ed. eadem (Zwolle, 1988), pp. 23-27.
50. ME I, pp. 241, 266.
51. SA 549, fol. 115r; J.C. Overvoorde, 'Gaaischieten 1473', *Leids Jaarboekje* (1910), pp. 123-125.

period the number of visitors and subsequently the costs of wine and meals decreased sharply. Moreover, the yearly distribution of wine on St. Martin's eve and on Corpus Christi was replaced by gifts of fixed amounts of money. Both on these occasions and with the gifts of wine to the Franciscans the character of the gift-exchange was modified: gifts in kind were replaced by gifts in money.

With the wine gifts the city tried first and foremost to increase its honour or reputation. Second, one expected that these material gifts were in one way or another returned to the city. This could happen in the same week, but also next month or even next year. As I have shown, the city authorities explicitly expected this countergift from officers of the prince. However, my data demonstrate that also in the case of the Franciscans an effective exchange of material goods and services took place.

The distribution of wine during political and religious festivities was essentially directed to the political elite of the city. As they were the most important actors both during the transfer of authority on St. Martin's eve and the procession on Corpus Christi, they benefited most from these wine gifts. In this way the cohesion of the political elite and the adherence of its defendants, the members of the shooting confraternities, were enforced. Moreover, the political order of the city was legitimised and communicated towards a broader audience.

Universiteit Leiden

Michael JUCKER

NEGOTIATING AND ESTABLISHING PEACE
BETWEEN GESTURES AND WRITTEN DOCUMENTS:
THE WALDMANN-PROCESS IN LATE MEDIEVAL ZURICH
(1489)*

Introduction

In spring 1489, a violent revolt took place in Zurich and its domains. Hans Waldmann, who had been mayor since 1483, was accused of bribery and of selling out Zurich's interests for huge sums of money. He was also accused of seducing the citizen's women and forging documents. These accusations and tensions between Zurich and its territory finally led to Waldmann's decapitation on the 6th of April. During and after the conflict, Swiss ambassadors came to Zurich several times and tried to intervene, negotiate the peace and calm the tumultuous situation. The unfolding of this conflict and its settlement will be the topic of this essay and serve as case study. We are aided in this endeavour by the fact that for various reasons the events are well documented in the sources.

Whereas earlier studies interpreted medieval diplomacy primarily in terms of a development towards conformity with the rule of law, and therefore as part of a general movement towards statehood and standardization, today the notion is slowly taking hold that diplomatic engagement and politics would be better illustrated as a cultural form with continuously changing political practices and flexible communication strategies.[1] The study of communication within conflicts has been a focus

* This essay is part of a project about diplomatic negotiations and peacekeeping in late medieval Europe, which was financed by the Forschungskommission of the University of Zurich and by the DFG-Projekt 'Verrechtlichung der Internationalität' former Sonderforschungsbereich 573 'Pluralisierung und Autorität in der Frühen Neuzeit' at the University of Münster, and is now continued in the Sonderforschungsbereich 496 *Symbolische Kommunikation und gesellschaftliche Wertesysteme vom Mittelalter bis zur Französischen Revolution* at the University of Münster.
    1. Rainer C. Schwinges and Klaus Wriedt, 'Gesandtschafts- und Botenwesen im spätmittelalterlichen Europa – eine Einführung', in *Gesandtschaftswesen im mittelalterlichen Europa des 13. bis Anfang des 16. Jahrhunderts*, eds. Rainer C. Schwinges and Klaus Wriedt, Vorträge und Forschungen, 60 (Stuttgart, 2003), pp. 9-14; Franz-J. Felten, 'Kommunikation zwischen Kaiser und Kurie unter Ludwig dem Bayern (1314–1347). Zur Problematik der Quellen im Spannungsfeld von Schriftlichkeit und Mündlichkeit', in *Kommunikationspraxis und Korrespondenzwesen im Mittelalter und in der Renaissance*, eds. Heinz-Dieter Heimann in Verbindung mit Ivan Hlaváček (Paderborn, 1998), pp. 51–89;

for many historians in recent years. Symbolic communication is becoming increasingly important.[2] The historical process of litigation and negotiation can be traced on different levels: between states, kingdoms, and enemies at war. At these levels, the *ius commune* and arbitration were constituents in bringing about peace. One can observe increasing diplomacy in all parts of Europe during the latter Middle Ages.[3] Peacemaking often involved a third party that tried to settle the conflict between two enemies.[4] Depending on the conflicts, these third parties could be papal

Martin Kintzinger, *Westbindungen im spätmittelalterlichen Europa. Auswärtige Politik zwischen dem Reich, Frankreich, Burgund und England in der Regierungszeit Kaiser Sigmunds*, Mittelalter-Forschungen, 2 (Stuttgart, 2000); Christina Lutter, *Politische Kommunikation an der Wende vom Mittelalter zur Neuzeit. Die diplomatischen Beziehungen zwischen der Republik Venedig und Maximilian I. (1495–1508)*, Veröffentlichungen des Instituts für Österreichische Geschichtsforschung, 34 (Vienna, 1998).

2. To mention just a few: Gerd Althoff, 'Beratungen über die Gestaltung zeremonieller und ritueller Verfahren im Mittelalter', in *Vormoderne politische Verfahren*, ed. Barbara Stollberg-Rilinger, Zeitschrift für Historische Forschung, Beiheft 25 (Berlin, 2001), pp. 53–71; Gerd Althoff. 'Die Veränderbarkeit von Ritualen im Mittelalter', in *Formen und Funktionen Kommunikation im Mittelalter*, ed. Gerd Althoff, Vorträge und Forschungen, 48 (Stuttgart; 2001), pp. 157–176; Gerd Althoff, 'Spielregeln der Politik im Mittelalter', Kommunikation in *Friede und Fehde* (Darmstadt, 1997); Barbara Stollberg-Rilinger, 'Zeremoniell, Ritual, Symbol. Neue Forschungen zur symbolischen Kommunikation in Spätmittelalter und Früher Neuzeit', in *Zeitschrift für Historische Forschungen*, 27 (2000), pp. 389–405. See also: Franz-Jozef Arlinghaus, 'Gesten, Kleidung und die Etablierung von Diskursräumen im städtischen Gerichtswesen (1400 bis 1600)', in *Kommunikation und Medien in der Frühen Neuzeit*, Johannes Burkhardt and Christine Werkstetter (eds.), Historische Zeitschrift, Beiheft 91 (München, 2005), pp. 461-498; Michael Jucker, 'Körper und Plurimedialität. Überlegungen zur spätmittelalterlichen Kommunikationspraxis im eidgenössischen Gesandtschaftswesen', in *Der Körper in Mittelalter und Früher Neuzeit. Realpräsenz und symbolische Ordnung*, Karina Kellermann ed., *Das Mittelalter*, 8, Heft 2 (2003), pp. 68–83; Michael Jucker, 'Gesten, Kleider und Körperschmähungen. Ordnungsbrüche und ihre Wahrnehmung im Gesandtschaftswesen des Spätmittelalters und der Frühen Neuzeit', in *Ordnung und Distinktion. Praktiken sozialer Repräsentation in der ständischen Gesellschaft*, eds. Marian Füssel and Thomas Weller, Symbolische Kommunikation und gesellschaftliche Wertesysteme, 8 (Munster, 2005), pp. 215-239.

3. See Kintzinger, *Westbindungen*; Petra Ehm-Schnocks, 'Praxis, Form und Inhalt. Diplomatie und Völkerrecht im Spätmittelalter', in Wulf Oesterreicher, Gerhard Regn, Winfried Schulze eds., *Autorität der Form – Autorisierung – Institutionelle Autorität, Pluralisierung & Autorität*, 1 (Munich, 2003), pp. 257–276.

4. Hermann Kamp, *Friedensstifter und Vermittler im Mittelalter*, Symbolische Kommunikation in der Vormoderne, 1 (Darmstadt, 2001); Christoph Kampmann, *Arbiter und Friedensstiftung. Die Auseinandersetzung um den politischen Schiedsrichter im Europa der Frühen Neuzeit*, Quellen und Forschungen aus dem Gebiete der Geschichte, 21 (Paderborn, 2001); Gerhard Dilcher, 'Friede durch Recht', in *Träger und Instrumentarien des Friedens im hohen und späten Mittelalter*, Johannes Fried ed., Vorträge und Forschungen, 43 (Sigmaringen, 1996), pp. 203–227; Elmar Wadle, *Landfrieden, Strafe, Recht. Zwölf Studien zum Mittelalter*, Schriften zur Europäischen Rechts- und Verfassungsgeschichte, 37 (Berlin, 2001); Norbert Ohler, 'Krieg und Frieden am Ausgang des Mittelalters', in *Krieg und Frieden im Übergang vom Mittelalter zur Neuzeit*, Heinz Duchhardt, Patrice Veit (eds.),

power, clerics, the emperor or the king. However, cities, local lords, and communes also played an increasingly important role within this process. In the late medieval Swiss confederation, ambassadors met in the Swiss Diets (*Tagsatzungen*) to pacify quarrels between the members of the confederation but also – since 1415 – to intervene in conflicts between subjects in the territories of occupied lands commonly administrated by the confederates, such as Aargau.[5] The envoys were representatives of the localities and most were members of both the local political communes and the ruling elite. Another important function of the Swiss confederates at the Diets was to mediate conflicts between European powers such as the Duke of Milan or the German emperor.[6] The Swiss Diets thus increasingly became international meeting points for ambassadors from all over Europe.[7]

At a lower level, peace was important as well. Various scholars have shown that the control of violence and its criminalisation within cities played an important role in state building.[8] Although one should not see in this a direct causal link and a continuous process from open violence to peaceful cultivated citizenship and stronger jurisdiction, it seems obvious that violence or the breaking of rules in towns and villages became increasingly stigmatised for various reasons. Among others, Susanne Pohl has recently shown that for Zurich peace among individuals (*Stallungen*)

(Mainz, 2000), p. 1. Cf. also: Reinhold Kaiser, 'Selbsthilfe und Gewaltmonopol. Königliche Friedenswahrung in Deutschland und Frankreich im Mittelalter', *Frühmittelalterliche Studien*, 17 (1983), pp. 55–72; Klaus Schreiner, '"Gerechtigkeit und Frieden haben sich geküsst". Friedensstiftung durch symbolisches Handeln', in *Träger und Instrumentarien*, pp. 37–86.

5. See now: Michael Jucker, *Gesandte, Schreiber, Akten. Politische Kommunikation auf eidgenössischen Tagsatzungen* (Zurich, 2004); Tamara Münger, 'Hanse und Eidgenossenschaft – zwei mittelalterliche Gemeinschaften im Vergleich', in *Hansische Geschichtsblätter*, 119 (2001), pp. 5–48.

6. See Jucker, *Gesandte*, p. 75; also: Andreas Würgler, 'Boten und Gesandte an den eidgenössischen Tagsatzungen. Diplomatische Praxis im Spätmittelalter', in *Gesandtschafts- und Botenwesen*, pp. 287–312.

7. See Jucker, *Gesandte*, pp. 13, 102, 123, 156; but also: Hans Conrad Peyer, *Verfassungsgeschichte der alten Schweiz* (Zurich, 1978); Roger Sablonier, 'The Swiss Confederation', in *The New Cambridge Medieval History, Vol. VII, c.1415–c.1500*, ed. Christopher Allmand (Cambridge, 1998), pp. 645–670.

8. See for example: *Köln als Kommunikationszentrum. Studien zur frühneuzeitlichen Stadtgeschichte*, Georg Mölich and Gerd Schwerhoff eds, *Der Riss im Himmel*, Bd. 4 (Cologne, 2000); Wolfgang Reinhard, *Geschichte der Staatsgewalt. Eine vergleichende Verfassungsgeschichte Europas von den Anfängen bis zur Gegenwart* (Munich, 1999); *Verletzte Ehre. Ehrkonflikte in Gesellschaften des Mittelalters und der Frühen Neuzeit*, Klaus Schreiner and Gerd Schwerhoff eds., Norm und Struktur, 5 (Cologne/Weimar/Vienna,1995); see also Gerd Schwerhoff and Andreas Blauert, eds., *Kriminalitätsgeschichte. Beiträge zur Sozial- und Kulturgeschiche der Vormoderne*, Konflikte und Kultur – Historische Perspektiven, 1 (Konstanz, 2000).

was strongly connected with the so-called *Stadtfrieden*, which meant peace in the city and the area within a town's jurisdiction. She emphasised that honour and symbolic capital were not only a question of individuals, but could also influence the jurisdiction, and that the relationship between the individual striving for peace and the *Stadtfrieden* was a complex system.[9] Most of the time peacemaking in such a situation was a matter for the town officials such as the council and the court, although other non-official forms existed until the early modern period.[10] Symbolic actions, literacy and law were crucial to litigation at the inter-state, trans-regional and communal level, and – although used concurrently – different media served different means.[11] Diplomacy and peacemaking can be seen as an ensemble of countless mutually-influenced factors such as writing, oral communication, secrecy, clothing, publicity, procedure, individual negotiations, and personal relationships. I have claimed elsewhere that these factors can be described as 'plurimedia' events with highly symbolic characteristics.

Whereas most historians focus *either* on the escalation of a conflict *or* its pacification, this essay will explore both aspects and discuss the situation after the conflict and its aftermath. The tumultuous incident of 1489 provides us with a good example of the use and misunderstanding of signs, gestures, and symbols. During the conflict and afterwards, symbolic communication was used to achieve several goals from different sides and parties. I would even claim that the use of signs and symbols led to an escalation of the conflict on the one hand, but on the other hand also helped to establish the peace later. These aspects were far more important than the juridical discourse. Therefore the main question is: What

9. See Susanne Pohl, 'Uneasy Peace. The Practice of the Stallung in Zürich, 1400–1525', in *Journal of Early Modern History,* 7 (2003), pp. 28–54. Pohl's study gives a good insight into juridical and illegal practice in Zurich and its domains, even though some place names are wrong, e.g. p. 46 resp. p. 50.

10. See Jucker, *Gesandte*; but for the rural hinterland of Zurich also Katja Hürlimann, *Sozialen Beziehungen im Dorf: Aspekte dörflicher Soziabilität in den Landvogteien Greifensee und Kyburg um 1500* (Zurich, 2000); for the city: Hans-Jörg Gilomen. 'Innere Verhältnisse der Stadt Zürich 1300–1500', in *Geschichte des Kantons Zürichs,* Vol. 1, eds. Niklaus Flüeler and Marianne Flüeler-Grauwiler (Zurich, 1995), pp. 336–389; Pohl, 'The Stallungen', p. 34; for Lucerne see: Elisabeth Wechsler, *Ehre und Politik. Ein Beitrag zur Erfassung politischer Verhaltensweisen in der Eidgenossenschaft (1440–1500) unter historisch anthropologischen Aspekten* (Zurich, 1991).

11. Bullard, Mellisa Meriam, 'Secrecy, Diplomacy and the Language in Renaissance', in *Zeitsprünge Forschungen zur Frühen Neuzeit,* Vol. 6, Heft 1–4, (2002) pp. 77–97; Valentin Groebner, 'Invisible Gifts. Corruption and the Politics of Information at the Beginning of the 16th Century', in *Zeitsprünge Forschungen zur Frühen Neuzeit,* Vol. 6, Heft 1–4 (2002), pp. 98–110; and also Jucker, 'Körper und Plurimedialität', pp. 68–83.

signs were used to achieve what goals, and in what contexts could they be understood properly and applied successfully?

Firstly, I will sketch the political situation in Zurich and discuss the reasons behind the rebellion; secondly, I will give an outline of the conflict and its settlement and thirdly provide an account of its settlement and the aftermath of the conflict. This will be done from the different perspectives of the participants, made possible by the various reports we find in the archives. I will explore the use and misunderstandings of symbols within the entire process, including the threat of violence, and the use of loud voices and gestures. The use of documents and their reference to traditions will be part of the discussion as well. I will not only examine the use of symbolic actions as a means to pacify the uproar, but also those actions that led to the conflict itself and expressed political intentions symbolically.

This will show how symbolic actions were engaged in to achieve certain political aims. It will also become clear that both sides of the conflict used symbolic language and referred to tradition as well. Because symbols can be ambiguously understood, at the end of this essay I will interpret the symbols and their use in the sources; this will also assist in avoiding the danger of establishing the wrong causal connections.

1. The political situation before the conflict

In the late Middle Ages, Zurich was always an important member of the Swiss Confederation. The city had been a powerful component of a treaty between the rural communities of Uri, Schwyz and Unterwalden since 1351, and later in other treaties with the town members of Bern, Lucerne, and Zug. Zurich, however, always maintained important relations with the cities of southern Germany and with the Habsburgs as well. The treaties within the Confederation mainly regulated mutual assistance between the different members in times of war; some of them also served as pacts and foresaw arbitration in conflicts.[12] The whole system, however, lacked a powerful princely leader to hold the political threads together and coordinate domestic and foreign policy. The individual members of the Confederation, the so-called *Orte* or localities, were self-sufficient communities or city republics. The entire assemblage can be

---

12. Still important: Emil Usteril, *Das öffentlich-rechtliche Schiedsgericht in der Schweizerischen Eidgenossenschaft des 13.–15. Jahrhunderts. Ein Beitrag zur Institutionengeschichte und zum Völkerrecht* (Zurich, 1925).

described as consisting of a legal conglomerate that grew out of the increasingly important *ius commune*. This bilaterally constructed system, however, did not purposefully develop into a state and the Diets were not foreseen in the treaties.[13] Until 1481, there was no unilateral system of treaties that encompassed all the localities.[14] Still, within this complex system of treaties and pacts, the Swiss Diets played an important role in the rule of common territories and the establishment of a collectively discussed foreign policy. For it was only since 1415 that envoys from the locality were required to convene in order to organize the administration of the new common possession and to solve additional supra-regional political problems.[15] The different members of the Swiss confederation, however, met only occasionally at Swiss Diets. Due to its ad-hoc and mainly political character, ambassadors came together only when it was necessary. The Diet had no common chancellery, no common archive and no common seal, which endowed it with a rather low level of centrality and almost no concentration of power.[16]

Instead, juridical conflicts between members were resolved by arbitration or more often by compromise.[17] Due to the autonomy of the individual members, ambassadors were rarely involved in internal conflicts between the authorities and their subjects.[18] The cities as well as the rural communes (*Länderorte*) did not allow others to intervene in their own politics.

As already mentioned, these *Tagsatzungen* increasingly became meeting points in which to search for trans-regional peace. Foreign ambassadors, however, also mingled with Swiss ambassadors and paid them pensions. This was stated explicitly by an envoy called *Judaica* in his missive from the Confederation home to the duke of Milan: 'Sine pecu-

13. See also: Dorothea A. Christ, 'Stabilisierende Konflikte und verbindende Abgrenzungen: Die Eidgenossen und ihre Bündnisse im Spätmittelalter', in Carl A. Hoffmann and Rolf Kießling (Eds.), *Kommunikation und Region*, pp. 139–161. See also Sablonier, 'Swiss Confederation'; Peyer, *Verfassungsgeschichte*.

14. Sablonier, 'Swiss Confederation'; see also: Ernst Walder, *Das Stanser Verkommnis. Ein Kapitel eidgenössischer Geschichte neu untersucht: Die Entstehung des Verkommnisses von Stans in den Jahren 1477–1481*, Beiträge zur Geschichte Nidwaldens, 44, Historischer Verein des Kantons Nidwalden ed., (Stans, 1994); Ernst Walder, 'Zur Entstehungsgeschichte des Stanser Verkommnisses und des Bundes der VIII Orte mit Freiburg und Solothurn von 1481', in *Schweizerische Zeitschrift für Geschichte*, 32 (1984), pp. 263–292.

15. Cf. Münger, 'Hanse und Eidgenossenschaft', p. 11; Jucker, *Gesandte*, pp. 75, 277–282.

16. Jucker, *Gesandte*, pp. 280–282.

17. See mainly Usteri, *Schiedsgericht*; Jucker, *Gesandte*, pp. 151, 235-239.

18. See Jucker, *Gesandte*, pp. 15–22, 236, 252; Münger, 'Hanse und Eidgenossenschaft', pp. 5–48.

nia nichil possumus'.[19] With money, on the other hand, a lot could be achieved at the Diets. In addition, foreign envoys lobbied at the urban and rural governmental committees, at times even secretly rounded up the mercenaries themselves and paid the authorities or the individual members the same pensions or attempted to bribe the political actors with donations and gifts. In return, the Swiss delivered the highly estimated infantrymen as well as important political information. This, of course, created tensions within the population. Rumours of corruption, denunciations and conspiracies spread throughout all the regions at the end of the 15th century.[20] The officials often were verbally accused of selling mercenaries for dirty money and that the mercenaries were simply slaughtered on the battlefields for foreign money. These signs of dissatisfaction with the rulers were not only uttered verbally; disturbances could also break out. Foreign money became a symbol of sin, poison and pollution of the body politic.[21] Some assemblies took place in a small town called Baden, which – in addition to its central location – was popular for its baths and brothels. Baden was the place where politics, bribery and sexuality came together. Thus in the eyes of rural population, Baden was the place of sin itself.

The ambassadors, however, were not keen to lose payments by foreign powers. The proclamation against the illegal practise of taking bribery or making money via mercenaries was left to those who did not share in elite power. Thus, the ambassadors established a monopoly to promote their own interests. It was mainly the cities that profited much: of course, not only Zurich but also Bern and Lucerne became the most powerful members of the Swiss Confederation during the 15th century. Zurich was always looked upon cautiously because Zurich's elite tried to

19. Berne, Federal Archives, copies from the state archive Milan (27.10. 1495) quoted in Ernst Gagliardi, *Mailänder und Franzosen in der Schweiz, 1495–1499*, Jahrbuch für schweizerische Geschichte, 39 (1914), p. 82.

20. See: Groebner, 'Invisible Gifts' and also: Valentin Groebner, *Gefährliche Geschenke. Ritual, Politik und die Sprache der Korruption in der Eidgenossenschaft im späten Mittelalter und am Beginn der Neuzeit*, Konflikte und Kultur – Historische Perspektiven, 4 (Konstanz, 2000).

21. Groebner, 'Invisible Gifts', p. 99; Jucker, 'Körper', p. 78. The economic implications of mercenaries are described in Hans Conrad Peyer 'Die wirtschaftliche Bedeutung der fremden Dienste für die Schweiz vom 15. bis 18. Jahrhundert', in Jürgen Schneider (ed.), *Wirtschaftskräfte und Wirtschaftswege*, Vol. II: *Wirtschaftskräfte in der europäischen Expansion, Festschrift für Hermann Kellenbenz*, Beiträge zur Wirtschaftsgeschichte, 5 (Stuttgart, 1978), pp. 701–716; see also: Hermann Romer, *Herrschaft, Reislauf und Verbotspolitik: Beobachtungen zum rechtlichen Alltag der Zürcher Solddienstbekämpfung im 16. Jahrhundert*, Zürcher Studien zur Rechtsgeschichte, 28 (Zurich, 1995).

break out of the Confederation several times and wanted to ally with the Habsburgs, especially during the so-called old Zurich war in the 1440s.[22]

As a *Reichsstadt*, however, Zurich's powerful and rich position also had its effect on its own Hinterland. Zurich's power lay in the hands of a few, mainly those who belonged to the councils. In fact, Zurich was ruled by artisan and trade guilds, which organised themselves into two councils and the *Konstaffel,* consisting of aristocratic families. From the *Grosser Rat* (large council) arose the *Kleiner Rat* which consisted of around 24 members; political power was concentrated within this small council and mainly consisted of a network around the mayor.[23] The most important institution of jurisdiction was the council court, which also judged in matters concerning the breaking of city peace. The city authorities bought and conquered many domains between the 13th and the late 15th century.[24] Zurich's council increasingly created its own administrative, fiscal and political infrastructure. The authorities organised their domains in communes and bailiwicks, which were required to pay taxes, served as military reservoir and were obliged to obey in all juridical aspects. Apart from Bern, Zurich had the greatest amount of land under its rule. Nevertheless, some parts or individual villages retained their earlier rights.

This situation worked quite well as long as Zurich did not encroach on these rights too much. This situation changed shortly before Hans Waldmann came to power. Waldmann's predecessors had already tried to force unification of rights onto the countryside. However, the attempt to centralise rights, abolish festivities in the countryside, forbid manufacture, and eliminate luxury, failed. Minor riots led to a retreat. The authorities promised that the villages could keep their traditional privileges.

---

22. Hans Berger, *Der alte Zürichkrieg im Rahmen der europäischen Politik. Ein Beitrag zur 'Aussenpolitik' Zürichs in der ersten Hälfte des 15. Jahrhunderts* (Zurich, 1978); Alois Niederstätter, *Der alte Zürichkrieg: Studien zum österreichisch-eidgenössischen Konflikt sowie zur Politik König Friederichs III. in den Jahren 1440 bis 1446*, Forschungen zur Kaiser- und Papstgeschichte des Mittelalters, Beihefte zu J. F. Böhmer, *Regesta Imperii*, 14 (Vienna, 1995); Christian Sieber, 'Die Reichsstadt Zürich zwischen der Herrschaft Österreich und der werdenden Eidgenossenschaft', in *Geschichte des Kantons Zürich* (see above nr. 10), pp. 471-496; Dieter Speck, *Die vorderösterreichischen Landstände. Entstehung, Entwicklung und Ausbildung bis 1595/1602* (Würzburg, 1994).

23. For an analysis of the council during Waldmann in power, see: Ulrich Vonrufs, *Die politische Führungsgruppe Zürichs zur Zeit von Hans Waldmann (1450–1489): Struktur, politische Networks und die sozialen Beziehungstypen, Verwandtschaft, Freundschaft und Patron-Klient-Beziehung*, Geist und Werk der Zeiten, 94 (Berne, 2002).

24. See Gilomen, 'Innere Verhältnisse'.

Waldmann became burgomaster in 1483. He obtained money and power via marriage and pensions.[25] Trade in iron and later in property also provided him with a good income. Of non-noble origin, he soon became aristocratic after being given a knighthood before a battle against Charles the Bold.[26] Waldmann received pensions not only from France but also from all the important lords in Europe.[27] He was estimated to be the richest man in the country. His income and political influence were enormous. Being mayor, pensioner and warlord at the same time caused tensions and envy throughout the country, among not only the simple population but at all political levels as well. It was due to Waldmann that the craftsmen's guilds increasingly gained power in the large and small council. He changed the constitution and replaced noble families with his own followers. In so doing, he managed to eliminate his direct opponent Heinrich Göldli, who was the former mayor and of noble lineage.[28]

That was roughly the situation before the uprising in 1489. We can detect three different areas of political conflict:

1st: the tension between the city and the countrymen in the villages, who asserted on their old rights;

2nd: the conflict between old noble families and Waldmann's network of craftsmen's guilds.

3rd: the more global fear in the Swiss Confederation that Zurich and Waldmann could become too influential and could betray the entire country in exchange for foreign dirty money.

In these special circumstances, conflict was predictable. Waldmann's stubborn character can also be described as marked by an eagerness for

25. Von Ruefs, *Politische Führungsgruppen*, pp. 176- 177.

26. See also Petra Ehm. *Burgund und das Reich. Spätmittelalterliche Aussenpolitik am Beispiel der Geschichte Karls des Kühnen (1465–1477),* Pariser Historische Studien, 61 (München, 2002). Arnold Esch, 'Alltag der Entscheidung. Berns Weg in den Burgunderkrieg', in *Berner Zeitschrift für Geschichte und Heimatkunde,* 50 (1988), pp. 3–64; Rogier Sablonier, 'Die Burgunderkriege und die europäische Politik,' in *Die grosse Burgunder Chronik des Diebold Schilling von Bern, 'Zürcher Schilling'. Kommentar zur Faksimile-Ausgabe der Handschrift Ms A5 der Zentralbibliothek Zürich,* ed. Alfred A. Schmid (Luzern,1985), pp. 39–51; Claudius Sieber-Lehmann, 'Burgund und die Eidgenossenschaft – zwei politische Aufsteiger', in Konrad Krimm and Rainer Brüning (eds.), *Zwischen Habsburg und Burgund. Der Oberrhein als europäische Landschaft im 15. Jahrhundert,* Oberrheinische Studien, 21 (Stuttgart, 2003), pp. 95–111; Claudius Sieber-Lehmann. *Spätmittelalterlicher Nationalismus. Die Burgunderkriege am Oberrhein und in der Eidgenossenschaft,* Veröffentlichungen des Max-Planck-Instituts für Geschichte, 116 (Göttingen, 1995); Norbert Stein, *Burgund und die Eidgenossenschaft zur Zeit Karls des Kühnen. Die politischen Beziehungen in ihrer Abhängigkeit von der inneren Struktur beider Staaten,* Europäische Hochschulschriften, Reihe III, Bd. 110 (Frankfurt a. M./Berne, 1979).

27. Vonrufs, *Politische Führungsgruppen*, pp. 176- 177.

28. See Gilomen, *Innere Verhältnisse.*

power. This might have had considerable influence on the process. Some researchers in the late 19th and early 20th century even considered Waldmann the first and last Machiavellian type in Switzerland.[29]

2. The 1489 rebellion in Zurich

There is no doubt that the 1489 rebellion was an extraordinary event in the history of the Confederation. This is evidenced not only by its political consequences or later accounts in chronicles, but also by the good archive documentation available. Thus, it makes sense to focus briefly on the sources before we take a closer look at this fascinating event.

Because Swiss ambassadors were involved in solving the conflict, we can rely on various reports. Normally Swiss ambassadors only gave an oral account of their role in conflict solving, or sent letters home.[30] The Waldmann Case, however, is different, not only because officials realised the importance of the event, but also because it was a long way to peace; thus, the different ambassadors could not return home to report immediately. The longest report can be found in the archives of Bern. It consists of more than 60 pages and must have been written down right after the pacification of the conflict. It is the official report from an ambassador to his council. Although it is labelled official and therefore somewhat apologetic – ambassadors had to show that they were successful – it is the most accurate account.[31]

From the perspective of Zurich there is also one unofficial account written by someone who was involved in the conflict. He wrote down his view a few years later, but we do not know who the author was.[32]

29. I will not go into the details of older historiography about Waldmann; apart from Gagliardi, most is myth building and only partly based on archival sources. See for example: Gustav H. Wunderli, *Hans Waldmann und seine Zeit* (Zürich, 1889). Still of good use is Otto Sigg, *Begleitschrift zur Ausstellung zum Gedenken an den vor 500 Jahren hingerichteten Zürcher Bürgermeister* (Zurich, 1989).

30. See also Jucker, *Gesandte*, S. 195–223, and forthcoming Michael Jucker, 'Trust and Mistrust in Letters: Late Medieval Diplomacy and its Communicational Practices', in *Trust in Writing, Papers from the fifth Utrecht Symposium on Medieval Literacy*, eds. Marco Mostert and Petra Schulte, Utrecht Studies in Medieval Literacy (USML) (Turnhout, 2006), in print.

31. The *Berner Bericht* is stored in the Berner Staatsarchiv, fol. 23–62 of the so-called Zürichbuch A, and edited in Ernst Gagliardi, *Dokumente zur Geschichte des Bürgermeisters Hans Waldmann*, Bde. 1 u. 2, Quellen zur Schweizer Geschichte, N.F. Abt. II, Bde. 1 u. 2 (Basel, 1911/1913), here Vol. 2, p. 333–388. Hereafter cited as Gagliardi, *Dokumente*.

32. The *Zürcher Bericht* is also edited in Gagliardi, *Dokumente*, Vol. 2, pp. 403–460. With some added material.

I should also mention a real gem: an anonymous report written by one of the countrymen involved in the uprising.[33] His report is clumsy, and accompanied by rather heavy-handed drawings. Nevertheless, the so-called *Höngger Bericht* is a document that reveals the perspective of rural people and how the background to the conflict as well as its development and termination were perceived from their point of view.[34]

Apart from the cited sources, we have much correspondence between the ambassadors and their authorities. Bern was keen to obtain sufficient information about the event. It organised a permanent system of messengers between the two cities during the conflict, mainly because it feared riots on its own territory.[35] Sometimes the authorities also complained that their ambassadors should write more news home.[36]

The conflict itself is characterised by continuing quarrels about power, status and political influence. The tensions between the rural population and the council of Zurich became more violent after Waldmann came to power. In November 1488, the council tried to centralise handcraft and trade in salt by forbidding it in the countryside. In fact, Zurich intended to monopolise both. The council also prohibited festivities, presents and excessive meals at weddings. Luxury, dancing, and baths were no longer allowed. Young men were banned from fishing in the lake. So-called *Gemeinden* – harmless political assemblies at the municipal level – were also prohibited. The new laws were written down in mandates concerning conduct and were read aloud in all regions of the territory. This of course, was a typical proclamation and served to provide the laws with stability by making them known to all.

Opposition from the countrymen was to be expected. While luxury was the symbolic capital of the leading elite of Zurich, and served as means of social distinction, countrymen were forced to renounce pleasures like bowling, and having their own spontaneous taverns, the so

33. The *Höngger Bericht* is edited in Gagliardi, *Dokumente*, Vol. 2, pp. 467–539 in two versions.

34. Concerning literacy and rural society, see: Thomas Meier and Roger Sablonier (eds.). *Wirtschaft und Herrschaft. Beiträge zur ländlichen Gesellschaft in der östlichen Schweiz (1200–1800)* (Zurich, 1999).

35. Gagliardi, *Dokumente*, Vol. 2, Nr. 274a. Concerning messengers, see also: Klara Hübner, '«Nüwe mer us Lamparten»: Entstehung, Organisation und Funktionsweise spät-mittelalterlicher Botenwesen am Beispiel Berns', in *Gesandtschaftswesen und Botenwesen*, pp. 265-286.

36. Gagliardi, *Dokumente*, Vol. 2, Nr. 265.

called *schenkinen*, the most important aspect of municipal political decision-making.

According to two reports, the straw that broke the camel's back – leading to the uprising of most villages – was an action performed by the council. In February 1489, it sent two officials to the countryside to kill the farmers' dogs, arguing that the dogs would damage the vineyards. They killed all the dogs in several villages until the officials were stopped a few days later by resistance in the south of the territory on the part of angry farmers who threatened the officials with sticks, pikes and their dogs.[37] The threat of violence was enough, and the dog hunters were forced to return to Zurich. Other villagers also assembled at the lakeside of Zurich, thinking the dog-killing would continue there. A couple of weeks later, countrymen also reacted with new actions against the new laws. In two villages, they broke the law against invitations and *Gemeinden* between men of the respective villages when they planned a meeting at the border and installed a barrel full of wine there to allow drinking from both sides. In one village, young men killed a wild boar, ate it with ostentation and publicly displayed its head on a pike.

Additional provocation took place at the political level. At a gathering in Erlenbach on Lake Zurich close to the city walls, about 4,000 people came together, a group the Hönnger account explicitly calls *Gemeinde*. In so doing, the farmers again broke the new laws. The countrymen planned not only to prevent further dog-killing but decided to send a delegation to Zurich to abolish the new restrictions because they infringed their traditional rights. However, the Erlenbach delegation was turned down by Waldmann, who told them to obey the new laws because they were for the common good.[38]

On the 1st of March, more than 1000 men came together in Meilen, an important village with many vineyards. The council of Zurich appeared to have learnt something from the past events and sent three delegates to Meilen, at first not to obtain the consent of the countrymen, but rather to find out who the plotters of the riot were. The delegates were confronted with silence. Finally, the parties decided that every village should send ten men to Zurich on the 5th of March.[39] This calmed the movement tem-

---

37. Concerning the stigmatised profession of dogkillers, see Franz Irsliger and Lassotta Arnold, *Bettler und Gaukler, Dirnen und Henker. Aussenseiter in einer mittelalterlichen Stadt*, 9th ed. (Munich, 2001), p. 272.

38. *Berner Bericht* (Gagliardi, *Dokumente*, Vol. 2, p. 334–335); also *Zürcher Bericht*, ibid, p. 407.

39. Ibid.

porarily, but not for long, because Waldmann made further mistakes. He now referred to juridical tradition. He was alarmed at hearing that an even larger delegation would arrive soon. He stubbornly referred to the old custom that only individual villages could present their petitions. Both sides of the conflict referred to tradition: the countrymen to their rights to assemble and to file petitions, and Waldmann to the tradition of only receiving individual villages or parishes. A solution seemed far away.

The conflict took a new turn when Waldmann decided to put armed sentinels on the city walls. The reaction was again the threat of violence. On the other side of the walls, thousands of armed countrymen assembled. Another delegation was invited to the council but was again turned down by Waldmann. He also denied them their traditional right of safe conduct on their return out of the city.[40] Furthermore, he came to know that the armed sentinels had already rebelled against him and opposition from noble families in Zurich was increasing. Violence was almost inevitable. Therefore, Waldmann, but also the countrymen individually, appealed to external help. Both sides wrote letters to the members of the Confederation, which then sent ambassadors to mediate in the affair.

The mediators were able to resolve the conflict within two weeks. A compromised settlement was finally reached: the countrymen were required to apologise for their uprising and would obey the council in the future, but in return the restrictions against traditional rights were abolished. Only the monopoly on the salt trade, taxes and the oath of obedience would remain. Waldmann and a councillor promised to comply with the settlement. It was written down in a document by the town chronicler. The countrymen had already departed from outside the city walls and abandoned their threat of violence. Peace appeared to be re-established through the help of the ambassadors and by compromise.[41]

Was it a stable peace then? Waldmann did not care much for the pledge he had made. The city-chronicler Ludwig Ammann read the new document aloud before the council, ambassadors and the farmers' delegates. However, Waldmann shouted at Ammann: 'Scribe, you have written wrong things. You should write that the countrymen begged us *humbly* for forgiveness for God's sake and in Mary's name, and we in return will forgive them their mistakes...'. Waldmann was obviously too

---

40. Concerning safe conduct, see now: Martin Kintzinger, 'Cum salvo conductu. Geleit im westeuropäischen Spätmittelalter', in *Gesandtschafts- und Botenwesen*, pp. 313–363.

41. Gagliardi, *Dokumente*, Vol. 2, *Zürcher Bericht*, pp. 410–413, *Berner Bericht*, pp. 338–339, *Höngger Bericht*, pp. 480–482.

proud to accept that the farmers had been successful and thought that the honour of the city had to be restored by describing the farmers as more humble. He wanted to change their apology into total subjugation. Thus, the scribe changed the text according to Waldmann's wishes, and handed the forged documents to the ambassadors and delegates, who did not dare contradict him and returned home.

Waldmann felt secure and victorious. He boasted that the countrymen were forced to beg humbly for forgiveness, and even bragged that they had to kneel down in front of the council. He had the forged treaty read aloud in all guilds. Then he went to Baden to celebrate his symbolic victory. However, this forgery and going to Baden – famous for its baths and brothels and the gatherings of bribing ambassadors – were clearly the wrong actions to celebrate. When the farmers heard about Waldmann's arrival in Baden and the forged treaty, they almost killed their delegates for not having intervened. The farmers wanted the documents to be torn to pieces immediately.[42]

Waldmann's journey to Baden and his boasting were another insult to the countrymen. According to the *Höngger Bericht,* it showed that Waldmann was not willing to fulfil his pledge.[43] New gatherings took place again. Young farmers wanted to go to Baden and retrieve Waldmann themselves. Having heard this, Waldmann quickly returned to Zurich on the 25th of March. There he had the city walls manned by sentinels again. The countrymen also reacted with occupation of several manor houses and a castle on the countryside. On the 28th of March, a delegation of the countryside did not reach a compromise before the council; they became angry and pillaged the town's taverns. In one of them, called Sternen, they spilt wine and took away fish.[44]

At the same time, assemblies took place outside of Zurich again. This time a delegation from the council came to them. As a member of the council tried to speak to the farmers from a small platform, some farmers yelled and threatened to throw him off the platform, symbolizing the will to overthrow the city's authority. Nevertheless, both sides concluded that the countrymen would remain calm until the ambassadors returned.[45]

However, trust in the political order was severely damaged, and in the city resistance increased as well. Especially people around the former

42. Ibid. *Berner* Bericht, pp. 341-342.
43. Ibid. *Höngger Bericht*, p. 486: 'Aber burgermeister Waldman(n) verachtent die ding und was ein stolzer man'. I.e. Waldmann denounced the things and was a proud man.
44. Ibid. *Zürcher Bericht*, p. 417; *Höngger Bericht*, pp. 491–492.
45. Ibid. *Höngger Bericht*, p. 492; *Zürcher Bericht*, p. 418; *Berner Bericht*, p. 342–343.

mayor Göldli had reasons to plan intrigues against Waldmann. He was forced to walk around with a coat of mail and dagger; his sentinels protected him day and night.

Finally, on the 31st of March, the ambassadors from throughout the Confederation arrived in Zurich. Waldmann invited them to the Tavern 'Sternen', the same place where the farmers had pillaged fish a few days before. Was it a coincidence? After lunch, Waldmann left the tavern at the very moment his convivial companion Schneevogel – who was hated and openly admitted that all the farmers should be killed – was stabbed to death by four people of Zurich. Waldmann tried to help him, but the ambassadors prevented his intervention, fearing he might be murdered as well. Later in the evening, Waldmann forgave the murderers with a handshake, intending to demonstrate good will between him and the killers. This, however, appeared to be the wrong gesture. The citizens interpreted it as a sign of Waldmann's lack of power. He did not realise the misunderstanding of his gestures.[46]

The next morning on April 1st, the ambassadors met in the Town Hall and ordered Waldmann to come there. The ambassadors wanted Waldmann and the council to delegate powers to allow them to resolve the conflict. Waldmann, however, did not give in immediately. The discussion dragged on and in the meantime, many armed citizens and countrymen came together in front of the Town Hall. They yelled and tried to break into the hall. The leader of the mass was Waldmann's archenemy, ex-Burgomaster Heinrich Göldli. Finally, he and a dozen men were allowed in to negotiate. They claimed that the township, and not the ambassadors, should resolve the conflict. Having aired this demand, Göldli and his fellows returned to the angry mass outside, which had grown ever larger. They yelled and wanted to put Waldmann and his friends in prison immediately, and again tried to enter with weapons.[47]

How was pacification in such a chaotic situation possible? The physical presence of the ambassadors hindered bloodshed. It seems that their active presence prevented the worst from happening and that they had a certain authority and – limited – power over the people. The ambassadors managed to calm the people with gestures like raising and lowering their hands and with loud shouting from outside the windows above. It worked, at least allowing negotiations to restart. In fact, in a compromise the

---

46. Ibid. *Berner Bericht*, p. 344; *Zürcher Bericht*, pp. 420–421; *Höngger Bericht*, pp. 494–496.

47. Ibid. *Berner Bericht*, pp. 345–347; *Zürcher Bericht*, pp. 425–428,; *Höngger Bericht*, pp. 496–498.

ambassadors promised to deliver Waldmann and his friends, bring them
to prison later, but that this act should not be done by the township itself.
On the other hand, they agreed that Waldmann should be brought to the
so-called Wellenberg, a tower in the middle of the river where normally
only rogues and rough criminals were kept. This of course was a con-
cession to the rebels.[48]

Some ambassadors had to intervene to prevent the crowd from breaking through the doors of the town hall while others negotiated with Waldmann. Realising that the crowd was getting bigger and bigger and that
there was the danger of a riot, the ambassadors turned to Waldmann
telling him that it was over. Quite shocked and now realising that he had
no chance, he tried to convince them that they had to help him, referring
to the above-mentioned old treaty of 1351. Some accounts report that he
even read this treaty aloud to all of the assembled ambassadors.[49] The
treaty between Zurich and some confederates contains a passage stating
that in the case of political danger, the other members should protect the
Bürgermeister and the constitution of Zurich. But this document only
included the rural members Uri, Schwyz and Unterwalden and not Bern
or Lucerne, and was drafted especially for the situation in 1351. One
could ask why Waldmann used an old document that was not valid for
all members of the confederation? And why use a document that no
longer corresponded to the political situation in Zurich? Interestingly
enough, it was Waldmann who had changed Zurich's 1351 constitution
several times for his own purposes. Moreover, why did he not mention a
treaty of 1481, the so-called *Stanser Verkommnis,* which would have
obliged the other Cities to intervene in such a situation?[50] It seems that
Waldmann referred to the older document for two reasons. Firstly, we all
know that old documents often have the aura of authority and of endur-
ing tradition. The old treaty might have served him as an emblem for the
old traditional solidarity between the members. Secondly, Rudolf Brun
who was mayor in 1351, was clearly an idol of Waldmann. Brun, like
Waldmann, managed to expel noble families and establish a constitution
led by guilds. By showing the document to the ambassadors, Waldmann
also referred to Brun as his ideal politician and an idealised situation.

However, the ambassadors were not impressed and decided to deliver
Waldmann and his friends, probably also because of the massive pressure

48. Ibid.
49. Ibid. The *Höngger Bericht* does not mention the juridical discussion about the
treaty, but it is mentioned in the *Berner Bericht*, p. 347. *Zürcher Bericht*, pp. 433–434.
50. Concerning the Stanser Verkommnis, see the works by Waldner as in footnote 14.

from the rebels on the street and because they were afraid that the riot could not be calmed otherwise.[51] Before bringing him out, the ambassadors removed Waldmann's dagger from him: another action demonstrating the deprivation of his power. Yet, it was not easy to bring Waldmann and the others to the prison, mainly because the angry crowd almost killed them. Here again the presence of the ambassadors prevented the worst from happening. They brought Waldmann and the other prisoners back to the Town Hall, and then had to negotiate again with the people on the street to find an arrangement that prevented them from killing Waldmann immediately. Armed ambassadors escorted the prisoner. As an ambassador of Lucerne wrote to his council, if they had not been there, there would have been a *Schlachtbank,* meaning a butcher's stall, the exact translation of the French word *massacre.*[52]

Having arrived in the tower, the citizens demanded that Waldmann be put into one of the lower cells where rough criminals were usually kept. However, the ambassadors denied this humiliating imprisonment. Two of them stayed to protect the prisoners, but not long enough. After two days, they abandoned the protection and the citizens put the prisoners into the lower cells: Waldmann into one with a sodomite where he was forced to eat from his cup, symbolising stigmatisation and deprivation of all honour.[53] This action was done not only to humiliate Waldmann but was also strongly connected to the above-mentioned pensions. Pensioners and bribing officials were often called sodomites and accused of voluptuousness.[54] It is no coincidence that the citizens accused Waldmann of sexual harassment of the wives of some citizens. Of course, these were only rumours. After Waldmann denied these and other accusations while being tortured in prison over the course of several days, they were not mentioned in the court again later.

The proceedings a couple of days later was not a juridical but rather a political action. Waldmann had no chance to defend himself against the newly established council, which consisted mainly of his archenemies from noble families like the family of Heinrich Göldli. All of Waldmann's network and friends had been expelled from the council.[55] The so-called *Hörnere Rat* was clearly ruled by Göldli and his friends, and even included people who did not have Zurich citizenship.[56] It was clear from

51. Gagliardi, *Dokumente,* Vol. 2, *Berner Bericht,* p. 348.
52. Ibid., Nr. 259. See also *Berner Bericht,* p. 348.
53. Ibid., mentioned in the *Berner Bericht,* p. 350; *Höngger Bericht,* p. 506.
54. Cf. Groebner, *Gefährliche Geschenke,* pp. 157–158; Jucker, *Gesandte,* S.265–269.
55. See also Vonrufs, *Politische Führungsgruppen.*
56. So claims Gagliardi, *Dokumente,* Vol. 1, 'Einleitung', p. CLXIV.

the beginning that he would be sentenced to death, although the court could not prove anything apart from the already mentioned forging of documents and that he had received money from different lords in Europe. These offences would never have justified a death penalty but only a fine and imprisonment. However, the new council also appeared to want to calm the farmers with Waldmann's death sentence. The revolting farmers still gathered around the city walls, occupied Waldman's house, celebrated ostentatious feasts and made strong demands for political participation in the city as well.[57] This frightened the new council and the demand of course was denied, but the council also tried to calm the situation by sacrificing Waldmann. It also seems probable that they wanted to prevent a later return to power by Waldmann. Rumours of troops arriving from Austria spread and at the same time three false messengers appeared in Zurich on 6 April 1489 with the intention of influencing the proceedings against Waldmann by bearing letters from the Habsburgs. To this end, they soaked their clothing in the river to create the impression they were covered with sweat from having travelled a long distance.[58] The ambassadors, however, did not intervene in this chaotic situation and totally abandoned their protection of Waldmann.

The execution and its aftermath

The execution of Waldmann was another highly symbolic act. On the 6th of April, early in the morning, the sentence was declared to Waldmann. He faced it with humility and then asked how he would be executed.[59] A friar, who was there to hear Waldmann's confession of sins, answered that he would be decapitated, and that he would be executed in front of the farmers, a fate which Waldmann humbly accepted, probably also because decapitation was an execution according to his high rank.[60] If he had been hanged, this would have been another form of dishonouring him. Waldmann confessed his sins for three hours, but not

57. According to all three reports.
58. Heinrich Brennwald, *Chronik,* Vol. 2, p. 314, quoted in Groebner, *Gefährliche Geschenke,* p. 90. See also the *Zürcher Bericht* in Gagliardi, *Dokumente,* Vol 2, pp. 451–452.
59. Ibid. The following is based on the *Berner Bericht,* pp. 356–357, the *Zürcher Bericht,* pp. 443–446, and the *Höngger Bericht,* pp. 508–512.
60. Concerning execution and rank, cf. Irsliger and Lassotta, *Bettler und Gauker,* p. 228–250; and also Jürgen Martschukat, *Inszeniertes Töten. Eine Geschichte der Todesstrafe vom 17. bis zum 19. Jahrhundert* (Köln, Weimar, Wien, 2000).

his crime.[61] Executions were always a public event and if something went wrong, it could lead to riots or uproars. Thus, everything had to be planned and organised carefully. This was also the case with Waldmann's execution. Different stages can be observed, with different symbols being used by several people. Before the execution took place, a kind of procession was organised which had to be public. After Waldmann's confessions to the friar, the bells of all churches in Zurich rang to announce the public part of the event. Many people gathered, Waldmann was taken from prison, the officials brought him to the riverbank; then a procession to the fish market took place where his golden chain that labelled him as a knight and burgomaster was torn off in public.[62] However, the execution did not happen in the fish-market. Another march took place. Waldmann was brought outside the city walls, conducted onto a small hill that was visible for thousands of the assembled farmers. During the journey, all the bells rang and Waldmann consoled his fellow prisoners by telling them to pray, and he asked the spectators to pray an *Ave Maria* for him. When on the hill, he himself prayed and asked for forgiveness. He made a cross with his foot on the ground, kneeled down and uttered the statement of faith; before he had finished it, he was beheaded.

However, the revolt did not end after the last performance of our hero. How was peace established after the execution of Waldmann? It took quite a while to calm the uprising in Zurich. This was only possible via the intervention of the ambassadors again. Fourteen ambassadors held discussions with every village and reached a compromise that protected the traditional rights of both parties. However, the envoys were not always able to persuade the farmers with words: sometimes gestures and even faked anger was necessary to convince them of a new peaceful solution.[63] Still, in the end a new peace was established and recorded in a document. We know from a diplomatic report that the established peace treaty was read aloud article-by-article.[64] It also seems very likely that this was the

61. Martschukat, *Inszeniertes Töten*, e.g. p. 37–42, among others including Michel Foucault, stated that there is a strong connection between the confession of sins and crimes in pre-modern Europe. In German, there is a differentiation on the linguistic level between 'geständig sein' and 'seine Sünden beichten', whereas in English and other languages a single term is used for both.
62. Concerning chains as signs of power, see also: Jucker, 'Gesten, Kleider'.
63. Concerning the faking of anger, see Jucker, 'Körper', p. 72–74, and Jucker, 'Gesten, Kleider'.
64. Gagliardi, *Dokumente,* Vol 2, *Berner Bericht*, p. 365.

case for most charters in the Swiss confederation as well. The structure
and content of some charters also indicate that the entire text was read
aloud. They often repeatedly refer to the consent of the parties involved
in establishing peace. I regard this emphasising of consensus before the
public in the texts as a measure to convince the audience of the stability
of the peace.

After reading aloud, several symbolic actions took place. Treaties and
charters were subject to another oath, this time not by the peacemakers
but by the citizens. This oath was also made in public, probably right
after or simultaneous with the promulgation. These general remarks about
oath taking regarding treaties can be found in many reports, which often
give accounts of festivities taking place around the oaths. This was also
the case in Zurich: the new peace was written down in nicely made documents and sealed by the ambassadors. The newly established order was
accompanied by a ceremony in tents on the so-called Lindenhof, the oldest part of Zurich. 2,500 people gathered; there was a good deal of eating and free drinking for everyone, music with drums and trumpeters,
and a procession through the town.[65] The ambassadors who established
the peace received 10 florins at the end of the ceremony.[66]

Villagers still had to swear an oath that they would obey the council,
but this oath was weaker than during Waldmann's regime. The farmers'
illegal possession of dogs was never mentioned again!

Conclusion

In making a conclusion, it seems obvious that different actors used different symbols to achieve several goals. However, symbols can be understood in different ways. Some symbolic actions are difficult to understand in a contemporary context. Was it a coincidence that Waldmann
invited the ambassadors to the same tavern where the farmers spilt wine
and stole fish the day before? Is there a certain parallelism between the
law against fishing and the fact that Waldmann's chain was torn off on
the fish market? The sources do not provide answers to these tricky questions and there are no direct connections between different actions. However, some symbolic actions seem to be of greater importance and resulted
in other actions; therefore their relevance can be better deduced, if not
completely ascertained. I call these actions symbolic actions because they

65. Ibid., p. 367 (28 May 1489).
66. Ibid., see also the calculations on p. 111 (4 June 1489).

refer to something else, to an underlying notion, just as symbols do. For example, the killing of the dogs was a symbolic demonstration of the authority of Zurich: not only demonstrating political power, but also showing who wields the power. It was not the damage the dogs did in the vineyards that was behind the killing, but the fact that Zurich would not tolerate the farmers hunting, a traditional privilege of the noblemen. Hunting dogs were even a symbol of nobility.[67] That the hunting obviously was a problem for the town's nobility is also mentioned in the established document at the end of the conflict.[68] The farmers' reactions can bee seen as merely symbolic. Since it was February, one could argue that the killing and eating of the wild boar was part of a Shrovetide ritual, but it had a politically symbolic meaning: the killing of the dogs was symbolically paid back by eating wild boar. The killing showed that the farmers were still able to hunt and kill game without their dogs. Above all, killing a wild boar, a game animal, also violated the privilege of nobles! The ostentatious eating of the boar also broke the law against extensive festivities. The presenting of a boar's head had a further political meaning. We can deduce from the agreement the farmers reached with the commune that the head of the boar had to be given to the bailiff in accordance with his authority. Showing the boar's head in public broke this law as well. Furthermore, it may be a bit farfetched, but it seems possible that the farmers also used the boar to show that they were rebellious and referred to a similar and earlier use of this symbol: in 1477 young farmers' sons from the rural parts of the inner valleys of the Confederation made a so-called *Saubannerzug,* a kind of raid against the authorities of the western part of today's Switzerland. They were violent and their banner depicted a boar. Only with many gifts and political concessions were the fearful authorities able to calm the situation.[69] The farmers of 1489 might have referred to this situation by showing the head of a boar in public on a pike and using a symbol of uproar. However, it would be too simple to say that only the villagers had an understanding for archaic or symbolic forms of communication, like the ostentatious eating of a wild boar as an answer to the killing of their dogs and as a provocation against the

67. Simon Teuscher. 'Hunde am Fürstenhof. Köter und "edle Wind" als Medien sozialer Beziehungen vom 14. Bis 16. Jahrhundert', in *Historische Anthropologie,* 6 (1998), H. 3, pp. 329–346.

68. Gagliardi, *Dokumente,* Vol. 2, p. 450. He claims that the document, now in Zurich, had been lost for a long time: Staatsarchiv: A. 43. But see a transcript of a copy on p. 575 where the killing of bears and boars is regulated.

69. Ernst Walder, 'Das torechte Leben von 1477 in der bernischen Politik 1477 bis 1481', in *Berner Zeitschrift für Geschichte und Heimatkunde,* 45 (1983), pp. 73–134.

new and unfair laws by Waldmann. The envoys and Waldmann used
symbolic communication as well. Waldmann's handshake with the murderers of his friend Schneevogel was meant as a gesture of reconciliation,
but was understood as a sign of weakness. Within the framework of diplomatic work, gestures or faked anger were also important and had nothing to do with a general law of diplomacy or even a *ius commune*, but
served to calm the people.

Symbolic actions were planned actions[70]: tearing off the burgomaster's
chain was a clear sign of loss of power. This of course was not a spontaneous act. Considering the fact that Waldmann had been tortured and
imprisoned, one can suppose that his chain was taken from him before
and again put on his neck later for edification of the public. Therefore,
we can conclude that this was part of a planned performance. By tearing
off the signs of power, the citizens publicly symbolised that Waldman-
n's power was definitely over. Although the loss of power had already
been effected, the public had to see the use of the right symbols to be sure
of it. The execution was also full of symbolic actions such as the singing
of the *Ave Maria*, the consolation of the fellow-prisoners by Waldmann,
the cross in the sand and the humble praying. Why this use of so many
Christian symbols and the public performance? Public executions were
important to calm the people and to show that the old regime had ended.
Jürgen Markutschat has recently shown that this was not always the case
and that it changed later in the modern period. Executions lost their performance and public characters over time. However, Christian symbolism
might have been used by Waldmann and his executors for different reasons. It is also possible that the symbols used could have been understood in different ways: whereas the executors might have emphasised the
just penalty and their authority, Waldmann might have tried to depict his
death as a kind of Christian martyrdom. This obviously worked: the mass
of blood that flowed out of him after he was beheaded was considered
extraordinary, and after his death rumours of his return spread; his grave
had a strange aura and chronicles of his life were produced as well.[71]

In general, we can state that symbols only worked at the right time and
at the right place, and understanding them depends highly on the political context and situation. However, symbolic actions must occur in public to develop a certain power and influence new actions. Only then can
symbols develop their own spheres of political communication. Symbolic

70. See the literature by Gerd Althoff on planned rituals.
71. See Gagliardi, *Dokumente*, Vol. 2, pp. 543-548 concerning the most important
chronicles; Martschukat, *Inszeniertes Töten*, p. 37-42.

actions could, but not necessarily, provoke new symbolic actions. Only in the first case, is it legitimate to speak of chains of symbolic actions that then can structure the unfolding of an event. Symbolic actions only become understandable for historians when we can put them into a broader context. As shown, symbolic actions were not the only means of communication. Both sides of this conflict referred to tradition as well. Some legal texts could then also become symbols for old solidarity and right order, and were preferred to newer ones.

Nevertheless, symbols were not always necessary in all situations, as shown in this essay. Often the mere presence of ambassadors could help to establish a peaceful situation. The final product, of course, was a written document with legal aspects and contents. Moreover, the farmers were well informed of their legal rights and were conscious of the danger of forged documents, as one can see in their reactions when the town's chronicler described them in the forged documents as too humble. Without doubt, the will to discuss problems was a first step towards peace. To send delegates was an important means to regulate discussions and to arrange reconciliation. However, agreements, calmed situations and final peace could only be achieved by finding a middle way, a process that was led by a third party such as the ambassadors. A third way also required compromise on both sides. Still, at this time we cannot yet speak of arbitration within states in the Swiss Confederation. Nevertheless, fragments appear to exist of normative and symbolic chains within such conflicts.[72] Some are based on norms as in treaties; others are based on non-written tradition. Although the 'Waldmannhandel' is not an example of a typical arbitration, it can be said for this case as well, that as soon as a third party is involved, peace seems nearer. The hostile parties' readiness for resolving the conflict already begins when they ask external people to help or intervene. On the other hand, the conflict discussed demonstrates the limits of a third party within such an event if the will to find peace is not there. If an open political situation is turning into violent revolt, even the presence of ambassadors could not always prevent further actions, be they symbolic, jurisdictional, political, or purely violent.

Wertfälische Wilhelms-Universität Münster

---

72. See Usteri, *Schiedsgericht*; Gerhard Rill, 'Arbitrium – tertia pars. Beobachtungen zur Völkerrechtspraxis der frühen Neuzeit', in *Recht und Reich im Zeitalter der Reformation: Festschrift für Horst Rabe* (Frankfurt a. M. /Berlin/ Berne/Paris/New York, 1996), pp. 97–119, especially pp. 98–100.

REGISTER

Montlhéry: 2
Morisis of Varsenare: 24

Nassau (family): 91
Nicolas Despars
Cronycke van Vlaenderen ende graefscepe van Vlaenderen: 2, 73, 75, 76, 79

Oath: 35, 36, 38-40, 67, 68, 70, 72-75, 120
Order of the Golden Fleece: 14
Otto of Grandson, Bishop of Basel: 30-41

Paris: 45, 48, 51, 52
Pas d'armes: 6, 14
Peace-agreement: XIV, 52-53, 120
Peace making: 101-123
Philip of Alsace, Count of Flanders: 19-20
Philip the Fair: 20, 69, 71, 73-74
Philip the Good: 1, 19, 24
Philip of Wassenaar: 94
Play: vide Abbeville
Pieter de Coninck: 20
Prisoners: 46-50
Pruntrut: 40
Public Encounters: XVII, 29-41
Processions: 2, 11-23, 25, 32, 98-99, 119, 120
Pyramus and Thisbe: 45

Rebellion: 65-83, 88, 101-123
Regnault Willems: 24
Reims: 46
Relics: 15-19, 25-28
Remi de Puys: 26
Rijnsburg (convent of -): 95
Roland le Fevre: 91
Rogation: 16
Royal entry: 43-64
Rudolf Brun, Mayor of Zurich: 116

Saint-Omer: 85
Safe conduct: 113
Schneevogel: 115, 122

Schwyz: 105, 116
Sermons: 17, 18
Silver: 85
Sluis: 23
Stadtfrieden: 104
Stallungen (peace among individuals): 103
St Basil (relics of -): 15, 16, 19, 25
St Francis: 95
St Donatian (relics of -): 16, 18, 19, 25-28
St George: 15
St John, feast of -: 38
St Martin's eve: 97, 98, 100
St Maximus: 15
Stedecannen: 84
Swiss Confederation: 105-108

Tableaux vivants: 1, 2, 11, 23, 26, 27, 50
Theatre-state: 3-9, 11, 12, 27
The Hague: 88
Tournai, abbey of St. Martin: 21
Townhall: 68, 75-76, 115

Underwalden: 105, 116
Urban V, Pope: 37
Uri: 105, 116
Utrecht (bishop of -): 95

(Le) Venite des Prisonniers du Chastelet de Paris sur la très-désirée entrée de la Royne de France: 51

Wassenaar (lord of -): 93
Wellenberg (Zurich): 116
White Bear Jousts: 1, 13, 15, 22, 24
William VI of Bavaria: 90, 99
William of Orange: 88
Wine gifts: 36, 37, 83-100

Ypres: 70-72, 74

Zug: 105
Zurcher Bericht: 110, 114-118
Zurich: 101-123
Zword (blessing of the -): 34

PRINTED ON PERMANENT PAPER • IMPRIME SUR PAPIER PERMANENT • GEDRUKT OP DUURZAAM PAPIER - ISO 9706

N.V. PEETERS S.A., WAROTSTRAAT 50, B-3020 HERENT